# FACTS AT YOUR FINGERTIPS

# GREAT SCIENTISTS
# LIFE SCIENCES

BROWN BEAR BOOKS

## Published by Brown Bear Books Limited

An imprint of:
The Brown Reference Group Ltd
68 Topstone Road
Redding
Connecticut 06896
USA

www.brownreference.com

ISBN-13 978-1-933834-45-0

**Editorial Director:** Lindsey Lowe
**Managing Editor:** Tim Harris
**Project Director:** Graham Bateman
**Designer:** Steve McCurdy
**Editor:** Derek Hall

Printed in the United States of America

# CONTENTS

*Page 1: Louis Pasteur.*
*This page: Edward Jenner.*

# CAROLUS LINNAEUS

## 1707–1778

*"I don't believe that since the time of Conrad Gesner there was a man so learn'd in all parts of natural history as he..."*

Jan Fredrik Gronovius
(1690–1762)

LINNAEUS LAID THE FOUNDATIONS FOR THE MODERN SYSTEM OF CLASSIFYING ALL LIVING THINGS. HIS METHOD, CALLED "BINOMIAL NOMENCLATURE," USED JUST TWO NAMES TO IDENTIFY EVERY SPECIES AND IS STILL EMPLOYED TODAY. HE IS REGARDED AS ONE OF THE GREATEST OF ALL NATURALISTS.

Carl Linnaeus was born in Råshult, Sweden, on May 23, 1707. The reason behind his name is interesting. Carl's father, Nils Ingemarsson Linnaeus, was a clergyman originally called Nils Ingemarsson (Nils the son of Ingemar), as was the custom in Scandinavia. When Nils became a student at Lund University, however, he had to add a formal surname in order to register. Latin names were fashionable, so he called himself Linnaeus after a type of lime tree ("linn" in the local dialect). When his son, Carl, began to publish his work, he took the Latinization further, calling himself Carolus Linnaeus.

Like many country parsons, Nils was an amateur botanist (botany is the study of plants), and it was through him that Carl acquired his enthusiasm for the subject. By the time he was eight years old Carl Linnaeus was already nicknamed "the little botanist."

### A MEDICAL EDUCATION

When Carl started high school, his parents hoped he would also become a clergyman. Linnaeus was a poor student, but he did become good at Latin. Johan Rothman, a local doctor and teacher, noticed Linnaeus's interest in plants and gave him private lessons in medicine and botany. Rothman encouraged Linnaeus to abandon theology and study medicine. In those days many medicines were derived from herbs, so botanical knowledge was useful. In 1727 Linnaeus enrolled as a medical student at the University of Lund, transferring the following year to the University of Uppsala.

### CLASSIFYING PLANTS

Uppsala University had a botanical garden, to which Linnaeus was soon drawn. It was there he met Olof Celsius, dean of Uppsala Cathedral and uncle of Anders Celsius (1701–1744), who devised the temperature scale that bears his name. Celsius, also a botanist, was

*Linnaeus's* Hortus Cliffortianus, *published in 1736, is examined by a group of characters in a painting by the Dutch decorative artist Jacob de Wit (1695–1754).*

impressed with Linnaeus's knowledge of plants, and introduced him to the garden's director, Olof Rudbeck Jr., who needed someone to take over from him. Rudbeck recognized Linnaeus's talent for the subject. Even though Linnaeus was only in the second year of his studies, the director invited him to become a lecturer in botany. Linnaeus was especially interested in flower structure. Developing the ideas he had acquired from Rothman, he was persuaded that it would be possible

## KEY DATES

| | |
|---|---|
| **1728** | Begins studying medicine at the University of Uppsala |
| **1732** | Mounts expedition to Lapland |
| **1735** | Graduates as doctor of medicine; publishes *Systema Naturae*, his classification of plants |
| **1739** | Appointed as first president of Royal Swedish Academy of Sciences; becomes physician to the Admiralty |
| **1742** | Becomes professor of botany at University of Uppsala |
| **1753** | Publishes *Species Plantarum* |

*Linnaeus wearing Lapp costume in a 1737 portrait by Martinus Hoffman.*

to introduce a new, much improved system for classifying plants based on their reproductive structures.

### TO LAPLAND

In 1732 Linnaeus set off on an expedition to Lapland, a wilderness inhabited by the Lapp people and extending over parts of Norway, Sweden, Finland, and Russia. He spent four months there, journeying hundreds of miles by foot to the Arctic Ocean, and discovering about 100 new species of plants. His account of the expedition, *Flora Lapponica*, was published in 1737. It was in this report that he used the alchemical symbols ♀ for Venus and copper and ♂ for Mars and iron to denote "female" and "male" respectively.

### LOVE BLOSSOMS

Linnaeus was keen on all aspects of natural history, and in 1733 lectured on mineralogy (the study of minerals) at Uppsala. In 1734, he traveled to the county of Dalarna to visit a copper mine. There he met a local doctor, Johan Moraeus, and his daughter Sara Elisabeth. Love blossomed, and he and Sara became engaged, though they did not marry until 1739.

Moraeus had qualified as a doctor in the Netherlands, and he persuaded Linnaeus to do the same. In 1735 Linnaeus graduated as a doctor of medicine from the University of Harderwijk. He then moved to Leiden in the Netherlands. There he showed one of his manuscripts to the botanist Jan Fredrik Gronovius (1690–1762), who was so impressed that he published the work, *Systema Naturae*, at his own expense. It contained a classified list of plants, animals, and minerals and aroused much interest among Linnaeus's fellow naturalists.

Linnaeus continued to travel around Europe. In 1737 he published *Genera Plantarum*, in which he expanded on his classification system for plants. The following year he visited Paris. He met many leading botanists, including the German Johann Dillenius (1687–1747), professor of botany at Oxford University

## BOTANICAL GARDENS

The botanical garden at Uppsala University was one of hundreds developed from the 16th century onward. The Renaissance that began in Italy in the 14th century brought a rebirth of interest in science, emphasizing the importance of very careful observation and recording; by the early 16th century European botanists were working with skilled illustrators to produce highly detailed books on plants, known as "herbals." In 1530, the German priest and botanist Otto Brunfels (c. 1488–1534) produced the first volume of his *Living Illustrations of Plants*, which marked the beginning of a more scientific approach to botany.

The interest generated by herbals in turn inspired universities in Europe to develop botanical gardens. The earliest, laid out in 1545, were at the universities of Padua and Pisa in Italy. Unlike most modern botanical gardens, which have plants for both study and ornament, these early botanical gardens derived from the medieval "physic" gardens (physic is an old word meaning medicinal), and chiefly contained herbs and other plants used in healing. University professors of medicine used these new botanical gardens both as an aid to teaching students and as a source of ingredients for making medicines.

*The University of Padua established Europe's first-ever botanical garden, shown here. There were estimated to be 1,600 such gardens in Europe by the end of the 18th century.*

in England, and French botanists, Antoine and Bernard Jussieu (1686–1758 and 1699–1777, respectively).

## DOCTOR AND SCIENTIST

Still just 31 years old, Linnaeus set himself up in practice as a physician. He was also admired for his scientific work. In 1739 he became a founding member and first president of the Royal Swedish Academy of Sciences, and was appointed physician to the Admiralty. In 1741 Linnaeus was first appointed professor of practical medicine at the University of Uppsala, but within a year he had become professor of botany.

As the science of botany became more established, botanical gardens were increasingly run by important botanists. In 1587 Charles de Lécluse, better known as Carolus Clusius (1526–1609), set up a collection of flowering bulbs at the University of Leiden; from this the Dutch bulb industry was developed. Just over 150 years later, in 1742, Linnaeus took over the supervision of Uppsala University's botanical gardens, which eventually contained about 3,000 species of plants.

Linnaeus made Uppsala the center of the world for botany. He also built a museum just outside Uppsala to house his huge collection of specimens. Today the botanical garden, Linnaeus's home, and the museum are all open to the public.

*A 15th-century illustration shows a medieval doctor selecting herbs to use in medical treatments.*

## PRESERVING THE PAST

The Linnean Society was founded in 1788, and is the world's oldest biological society. Its first president was Sir James Edward Smith (1759–1828), an English medical student and naturalist. In 1783, Smith bought Linnaeus's vast collection of manuscripts and specimens from Linnaeus's widow in Sweden; she needed the money to provide dowries for her four daughters. Smith initially rented rooms in London in which he displayed the collection to a curious public.

The first meeting of the Linnean Society was held at Smith's home on April 8, 1788, its aim "the cultivation of the science of Natural History." The society remains a key forum for discussion on many aspects of science. In 1829, after Smith's death, the society bought the Linnean and the Smith collections and libraries, though the purchase plunged it into debt for 30 years. More than 40,000 specimens from Linnaeus's collection are preserved in its London headquarters, alongside several other major plant and animal collections. The society also houses an important library specializing in works on the classification system that Linnaeus so successfully standardized.

*The title page of Volume III of a 1768 edition of* Systema Naturae, *and the frontispiece of* Hortus Cliffortianus *(1736). Many of Linnaeus's books, travel diaries, and manuscripts have been preserved by the Linnean Society.*

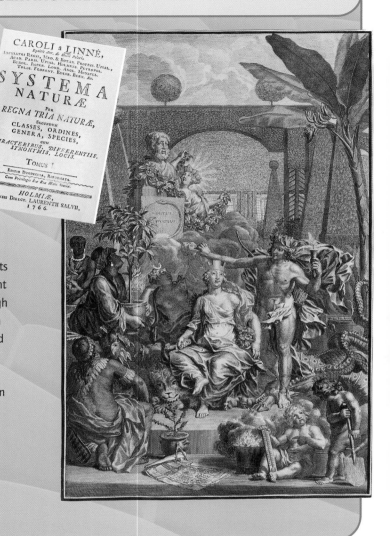

### LINNAEUS'S LEGACY

*Species Plantarum*, published in 1753, is considered to be Linnaeus's most important work, listing all the species known at the time according to his system of classification. The system was easy to use, enabling people to categorize species quickly. Together with the fifth edition (1754) of *Genera Plantarum*, *Species Plantarum* remains to this day the starting point for botanical nomenclature of flowering plants and ferns.

Linnaeus published about 180 books. He urged his students to visit every part of the world in search of new specimens. Twenty-three of his former students became professors; they helped Linnaeus spread his ideas to the leading European naturalists of the day. The king and queen of Sweden were among his patrons, and in 1761 he was made a nobleman. From then on he was known as Carl von Linné.

In 1774 Linnaeus suffered a stroke. He died at Uppsala on 22 January, 1778, and was buried in the cathedral. His son succeeded him in his post as professor of botany at Uppsala University, continuing to add to his father's unique collection.

# CAROLUS LINNAEUS

1700     1730     1760     1780

## SCIENTIFIC BACKGROUND

**Before 1700**

Aristotle (384–322 BC) makes a systematic study of plants and animals

English naturalist John Ray (1627–1705) classifies animal species into groups by their toes and teeth

Swiss botanist Caspar Bauhin (1560–1624) publishes a compendium of all known plants (*Pinax Theatri Botanici*)

**1721** The German botanist Rudolph Camerarius (1665–1721) dies. Director of the botanic garden at Tübingen, he gained proof of sexuality in plants

**1727** English botanist and chemist Stephen Hales (1677–1761) publishes *Vegetable Staticks*, on the physiology of vegetables

**1737** In *Genera Plantarum*, Linnaeus expands on his plant classification system

**1738** *Ichthyology*, a systematic study of fishes by Peter Artedi (1705–1735), is published posthumously

**1742** Linnaeus becomes professor of botany at Uppsala University

**1749** George-Louis Leclerc, Comte de Buffon (1707–1788), begins his 44-volume *Natural History*

**1753** Linnaeus publishes *Species Plantarum*, in which he lists and classifies all known species of plants

**1754** Swiss naturalist and philosopher Charles Etienne Bonnet (1720–1793) publishes his *Study on the Use of Plant Leaves*

**1771** English naturalist Joseph Banks (1743–1820) returns from his epic voyage to the southern hemisphere with Captain James Cook (1728–1779); he brings back 800 previously unknown species of plants

**1771** Joseph Banks is appointed director of the botanic gardens at Kew, in London

**1788** The first meeting of the Linnean Society takes place in London

**After 1800**

**1800–1812** French naturalist Georges Cuvier (1769–1832) extends Linnaeus's classification system

**1858** English naturalist Charles Darwin (1809–1882) announces his theory of evolution at the Linnean Society

## POLITICAL AND CULTURAL BACKGROUND

**1700** The Great Northern War begins between Sweden and Russia; it lasts until 1721 when Russia gains Swedish lands in the Baltic

**1703** Peter the Great (1672–1725), tsar of Russia, founds the city of St. Petersburg as his northern capital

**1725** English writer Jonathan Swift (1667–1745) publishes *Gulliver's Travels*

**1742** George Friederic Handel (1685–1759) completes his oratorio, *The Messiah*, which receives its first performance in Dublin, Ireland

**1751** French writer Denis Diderot (1713–1784) publishes the *Encyclopedia*, a key work of the Enlightenment

**1755** Lisbon, capital of Portugal, is destroyed in a devastating earthquake

**1762** Catherine the Great (1729–1796) becomes empress of Russia

**1768–71** Captain James Cook makes his first Pacific voyage, discovering New Zealand and Australia

**1774** The first Shakers colony is founded in the United States; the Christian group is an offshoot of the Quakers

**1776** The American Declaration of Independence is signed on July 4

**1788** The *Times* newspaper is founded in London

**1789** The French Revolution begins

# EDWARD JENNER

## 1749–1823

**"[Man] has familiarized himself with a great number of animals, which may not originally have been intended for his associates."**

Edward Jenner
*An Inquiry into the Causes and Effects...
of the Cow Pox*
(1798)

Edward Jenner is the man who helped save the lives of millions of humans by preventing a terrible disease. Indirectly, he also laid the foundations for virology (the study of viruses).

Jenner was born on May 17, 1749, in Berkeley, Gloucestershire, England. In 1770 Jenner traveled to London to study surgery and anatomy (the physical structure of animals and plants) under the Scottish surgeon John Hunter (1728–1793). While in London, Jenner was also employed by the naturalist Sir Joseph Banks (1743–1820), who had sailed with the British explorer Captain James Cook (1728–1779), as the official naturalist on Cook's first expedition to the southern hemisphere, from 1768 to 1771. Jenner helped Banks sort the specimens he had collected.

In 1773 Jenner returned to Berkeley, where he stayed for the rest of his life. He set up practice as a physician, and in 1788 married Catharine Kingscote. In 1792 he was awarded the degree of doctor of medicine by the University of St. Andrews in Scotland.

### A RISKY TREATMENT

In the 18th century smallpox was a common and much feared disease. Many died during smallpox epidemics. At this time the only method of fighting the disease was inoculation. Inoculation involves implanting a mild form of a disease in a healthy person in order to build up a resistance. In the case of smallpox, "matter" from the blisters on a person with a mild attack was injected into the patient. But inoculation was risky: the inoculated patient could get a serious, even fatal dose, or could pass on the infection to other people.

### COWPOX AND FOLKLORE

By 1775 Jenner had become interested in smallpox and its link with cowpox, a similar disease, but much less

*The romantic 19th-century painting* The Vaccination, *by the French artist Constant Joseph Desbordes (1761–1827), depicts Jenner's work.*

severe. It affects cows, and milkmaids often caught it from milking infected cows. People had known for centuries that anyone who survived smallpox never caught it again, and that even the mildest infection made them resistant to the disease, or "immune." There was a folk belief in Gloucestershire that cowpox sometimes had the same effect, giving those who had suffered it immunity against smallpox.

Jenner found that there are two forms of cowpox, but only one protects against smallpox. He also found that cowpox only protects against smallpox if a person

## KEY DATES

| | |
|---|---|
| **1770** | Becomes a student of surgeon John Hunter |
| **1773** | Returns to Berkeley and becomes a successful physician |
| **1775** | Conducts first investigation of cowpox |
| **1788** | Smallpox epidemic breaks out in Gloucestershire |
| **1796** | May 14, inoculates James Phipps using matter from cowpox pustules; in July exposes Phipps to smallpox with no ill effect |
| **1798** | Second trial proves successful; Jenner publishes his findings and coins the word "vaccination" |
| **1803** | 12,000 Londoners are vaccinated in 18 months |

# EDWARD JENNER

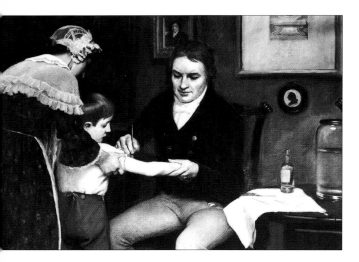

*Edward Jenner injecting eight-year-old James Phipps with infected cowpox matter in 1796 to prevent him from contracting smallpox.*

gets it at the right stage in its development. Jenner found, too, that exposure to a disease of horses called "the grease," also gave people immunity to smallpox.

In 1788 Jenner's home county was struck by a smallpox epidemic. As Jenner traveled about, treating patients in the traditional way, he was struck again by the fact that people who had suffered from cowpox in the past did not show symptoms of smallpox, despite being exposed to it. He suspected that inoculation with cowpox would be an effective and safer form of preventive medicine than inoculation with live smallpox.

## A MILKMAID LENDS A HAND

As luck would have it, there were few cowpox cases in Gloucestershire at that time, but in 1796 Jenner found a milkmaid with the telltale blisters on her hands. On May 14, 1796, he performed the first inoculation with cowpox on a patient, a boy called James Phipps. Jenner made small cuts in James's arm and worked into them a small amount of material from the milkmaid's blisters. James suffered a mild fever, but soon recovered. In July Jenner inoculated James again, but this time with matter from a smallpox victim. James remained healthy.

Jenner repeated the experiment in 1798. The second trial was also successful, and Jenner reported his findings to the Royal Society. Some members of the

## A DEADLY HISTORY

No one knows when smallpox first infected humans. It was recognized in Africa and Asia by around 1000 BC. An Egyptian mummy from the 20th dynasty (1200–1100 BC) has marks on the skin that were caused by smallpox. The disease probably reached Europe in the 6th century. In 570 AD Bishop Marius of Avenches called the illness "variola," which is Latin for "pox," and this became its scientific name.

Those who survived smallpox could often be disfigured and blinded by it. Many were pockmarked, their bodies and especially their faces covered with scars and pits marking the places where there had been blisters. In extreme cases pockmarks could almost destroy faces.

The early symptoms of smallpox are similar to those of other pox diseases, especially chickenpox and measles. It begins with fever, chills, nausea, and aching, followed by the appearance of painful, swollen blisters. It takes about 12 days after a person is infected for the disease to become evident. During that time the infection passes very readily through droplets from the nose and mouth, released by coughing and sneezing. Later, anyone touching the patient's blisters, scabs, bedding, or even objects just handled

*An etching of the hand of the milkmaid Sarah Nelmes, complete with the cowpox pustules from which Jenner made his first vaccine.*

society were critical of his report, believing in inoculation using infected smallpox matter. They advised Jenner not to risk his reputation by challenging the established opinion. So Jenner published his paper privately under the title, *Inquiry into the Causes and Effects of the Variolae Vaccinae.*

by them could become infected. The effect of smallpox on people never before exposed to it could be devastating. In 1519 the Spanish conquistadors brought the disease to Mexico, where it killed 3.5 million Mexican Indians. Later, entire tribes of Native North Americans died of smallpox after encounters with European colonists.

## Traditional Healing

Chinese healers had long known it was possible to make people immune to particular diseases by having them catch them from patients suffering mild attacks, or by rubbing in infected material from victims. This practice, a form of inoculation, reached Turkey by the

18th century, and it was taken to western Europe soon afterward, probably by Lady Mary Wortley Montagu (1689–1762), who had lived in Turkey as the wife of the British ambassador there. The technique was not commonly used, though; it was only with the introduction of Jenner's vaccination that a wider public began to benefit from the protection of an injection.

*Fable and fact: Heroic Japanese archer Tametomo tries to drive away smallpox demons in this 19th-century print (left), and the grim realities of a ward in a London smallpox hospital around 1820 (below).*

"Vacca" is the Latin name for cow; from this Jenner coined the word "vaccination" to describe inoculation with cowpox matter. Inoculation with smallpox (variola) matter is known as "variolation." Although Jenner had found a way to protect people against smallpox, he had no idea why it worked. That discovery came much later.

## VACCINATION SAVES MANY LIVES

Within a few years vaccination was being practiced widely. In 1802 Parliament awarded Jenner a large grant to help his work. Jenner vaccinated the poor free of charge. A Royal Jennerian Society was established in 1803 to promote vaccination in London; the average annual death rate from smallpox in London fell from 2,018 to 622. The Royal College of Physicians reported favorably on vaccination in 1807, and the British government was moved to increase Jenner's grant.

Jenner became famous worldwide. In parts of Germany his birthday was made a holiday. The French emperor Napoleon Bonaparte (1769–1821) was impressed by Jenner's work. When some British civilians were captured by the French, a petition for their release was delivered to Napoleon. Because Jenner was among those who had signed it, Napoleon freed the prisoners.

Britain was relatively slow to recognize Jenner's achievement, though the University of Oxford awarded him an honorary doctorate of medicine in 1813. Jenner published his last work on vaccination in 1822.

Jenner died from a stroke on January 26, 1823.

## Jan Ingenhousz
### 1730–1799

Jan Ingenhousz was a Dutch physician and plant physiologist who introduced the technique of variolation to London. This was the process of inoculation using smallpox matter. It proved successful in many cases. He opposed Jenner's championing of vaccination as an alternative. Ingenhousz went to Vienna in 1768 to inoculate the royal family and was made court physician. In 1779 he returned to London, and in the same year discovered the principles of photosynthesis, the process whereby green plants absorb carbon dioxide by day and give it out at night.

## SMALLPOX ERADICATION

Scientists now know that smallpox (variola) is spread by a virus. The variola virus has one weakness: it can live and multiply only in humans. So if the virus could be eliminated from the human population, smallpox would be "eradicated." This word means it would disappear for ever, and is from the Latin word meaning "to uproot."

Smallpox vaccination programs had already made smallpox a rare disease in Europe, North America, Australia, and New Zealand. But in countries that could not afford to vaccinate everyone, the disease was still common. So in 1967 the World Health Organization (WHO), an agency of the United Nations, launched a World Eradication Program against the disease. Vaccination programs were to be made available all over the world, and all governments were asked to report any smallpox cases in their countries.

Success came swiftly. In 1966, the year before the program started, in the world as a whole between 10 and 15 million people had died from smallpox. Within a decade the number of cases had fallen

*The last endemic smallpox carrier in the world was Ali Maow Maalin, of Merka, Somalia.*

dramatically. The last recorded case due to natural infection was in the African country of Somalia, in 1977.

In 1979 the WHO declared smallpox to have been eradicated throughout Africa, and in 1980 it was able to announce that the disease had been completely eliminated throughout the world. However, small stocks of the virus were still held in medical laboratories for purposes of research. The WHO recommended that all such stocks be destroyed by 1999 because of the dangers of laboratory workers being exposed to the virus and causing outbreaks of the disease. It is possible that some stocks are still held illicitly because of their potential for use as a biological weapon, but officially smallpox no longer exists.

# EDWARD JENNER

## SCIENTIFIC BACKGROUND

**Before 1760**

The mummified body of Egyptian pharaoh Ramses V (died c. 1156 BC) shows symptoms of smallpox

Smallpox is known to exist in Africa and Asia around 1000 BC; it is also referred to in Sanskrit texts of India

In c. 570 AD, Bishop Marius of Avenches calls the illness "variola," from the Latin word for "pox"

Persian physician Rhazes, or Al-Razi (864–930 AD), distinguishes between the symptoms of smallpox and measles

**1761** Jenner is apprenticed to the surgeon Daniel Ludlow

**1765** Dutch physician Jan Ingenhousz (1730–1799) moves to London and begins "variolation"

**1767** English physician William Heberden (1710–1801) distinguishes between smallpox and chickenpox

**1774** Jenner's teacher, Scottish surgeon John Hunter (1728–1793), publishes *Anatomy of the Human Gravid Uterus*, his greatest work on anatomy

**1775** Jenner conducts first investigation into cowpox

**1796** Jenner vaccinates James Phipps on May 14; in July he exposes Phipps to smallpox with no effect

**1798** Jenner's second trial using cowpox vaccination proves successful; he publishes his findings

**1802** Boston's Board of Health orders vaccination against smallpox on the recommendation of Harvard medical professor Benjamin Waterhouse (1754–1846)

**1807** Royal College of Physicians reports favorably on vaccination; Jenner receives increased grant

**1813** University of Oxford awards Jenner an honorary doctorate of medicine

**1822** Jenner publishes his last work on vaccination

**After 1850**

**1967** The World Health Organization (WHO) launches its World Eradication Program against smallpox

**1977** The last naturally occurring case of smallpox is recorded

**1979** Smallpox is eradicated throughout Africa

**1980** Smallpox is eradicated worldwide

---

**1750**    **1760**    **1790**    **1820**

---

## POLITICAL AND CULTURAL BACKGROUND

**1755** The first ever *Dictionary of the English Language*, by the English lexicographer and writer Dr Samuel Johnson (1709–84), is published

**1770** Fighting between British troops and colonists leaves three people dead in what becomes known as the Boston Massacre

**1778** France recognizes American independence; in 1779 Spain will also pledge support for the colonists in their war against Britain

**1783** Congress declares victory in the American War of Independence

**1789** As revolution takes hold in France, the French assembly announces its Declaration of the Rights of Man; they include the right to free speech

**1792** Francis II (1768–1835) becomes the last Holy Roman emperor after the death of his father, Leopold II (1747–1792). The empire is abolished by the French ruler Napoleon Bonaparte (1769–1821) in 1806

**1808** The United States outlaws involvement in the trade of slaves, but allows ownership of slaves to continue until 1865

**1815** Napoleon is defeated at the battle of Waterloo in Belgium on June 18, and abdicates four days later

**1825** English-born American artist Thomas Cole (1801–1848) founds the Hudson River school of art, specializing in paintings of the unspoiled wildernesses around the Hudson River and Catskill Mountains in New York State

# CHARLES DARWIN

## 1809-1882

*"Can we doubt (remembering that many more individuals are produced than can possibly survive) that individuals having any advantage, however slight, over others, would have the best chance of surviving and of procreating their kind?"*

Charles Darwin
*On the Origin of the Species*
(1859)

CHARLES DARWIN, TOGETHER WITH ALFRED RUSSEL WALLACE, SHOWED HOW THE CHARACTERISTICS OF SPECIES MIGHT DEVELOP OVER LONG PERIODS OF TIME. THE PROPOSAL, KNOWN AS THE THEORY OF EVOLUTION BY NATURAL SELECTION, WAS TO REVOLUTIONIZE HOW PEOPLE VIEWED THE WORLD AND THEMSELVES.

Charles Darwin was born in Shrewsbury, England, on February 12, 1809. He showed an early interest in science, and in 1825 he went to study medicine at the University of Edinburgh. But, despite being the son and grandson of doctors, he disliked the subject. Darwin also studied theology at Cambridge University for a time, but his real interest was natural history. While at Cambridge he met many eminent scientists. One, Adam Sedgwick (1785-1873), was professor of geology. In 1831 Darwin accompanied Sedgwick on a field excursion to Wales—the only time Darwin ever received formal scientific training.

Darwin graduated in 1831 without immediate plans to become a clergyman. Meanwhile in London, Robert Fitzroy (1805-65), captain of HMS *Beagle*, was preparing an expedition to survey the coasts of South America for the Royal Navy, and he advertised for a "well-educated and scientific person" to join the voyage. Darwin applied for the post and was duly chosen.

### THE BIRTH OF A NEW SCIENCE

Until the 18th century, people believed that the Earth was only a few thousand rather than millions of years old. However, some scientists speculated that the Earth's history was much longer. In 1795 Scottish scientist James Hutton (1726-97) suggested that the Earth had changed very slowly over millions of years, and was still changing. This theory led to the creation of a new science, geology—the study of the origin, history, structure, and makeup of the Earth.

By the early 19th century Scottish geologist Charles Lyell had reached the same conclusion as Hutton. Hutton and Lyell's theories met with strong resistance; Darwin was advised to read "but not believe" the first volume of Lyell's book, *Principles of Geology* (1830). But Darwin was greatly impressed by the book, and what he

# LAYERS OF HISTORY

Until the coming of modern dating techniques, scientists could not tell the age of rocks; they just had to rely on deciding in which order rocks had been formed so that they could try and understand how the Earth had developed. We now know that sediments are laid down in layers, known as strata (singular, stratum). Danish physician Nicolaus Steno (1638–1686) was the first person to recognize this; his Principle of Superposition states that, in an undisturbed sequence of sedimentary rocks (rocks made from sediments), the oldest strata lie at the bottom and the youngest at the top. However, there was a problem: in any places where the strata were disturbed—by earth movements or erosion, for example—this rule could not apply.

While studying strata in England, William Smith (1769–1839) found that each layer contained a different collection, or "assemblage," of fossil remains of extinct plants and animals. He realized that this information could be used to confirm the order in which rocks had formed; geologists could identify the relative age of particular strata by the assemblage of fossils they found in them. Combining this information with the Principle of Superposition, Smith was able to build up the first geological map of England, which was published in 1815. This showed rock sequences colored according to their age.

Scottish geologist Charles Lyell (1797–1875), shown above left, was fascinated by these attempts to date rock; he was convinced that the Earth had developed slowly over a very long time. His *Principles of Geology* (1830–33) and *Elements of Geology* (1838) gave examples from his surveys of European rocks and fossils, showing that the processes that had changed the Earth in the past were continuing still.

*Darwin was secretary of the Geological Society from 1838 to 1841. It mapped Britain's rock strata, such as these sections of a river cliff in England, drawn by the first director of the Society's geological survey, Henry de la Beche (1796–1855).*

saw over the months and years of the *Beagle*'s trip persuaded him that Lyell's theories were correct.

## CHANGING PLANTS AND ANIMALS

Christians also believed that God had made animals and plants in a "Great Chain of Being," at the top of which was mankind. By the end of the 18th century, some people were questioning these views. Among them was Charles's grandfather, Erasmus Darwin (1731–1802), and several French scientists. The Chevalier de Lamarck (Jean Baptiste Pierre Antoine de Monet, 1744–1829) was a French naturalist. He proposed a way in which species might change.

## KEY DATES

| | |
|---|---|
| **1825–28** | Studies medicine at Edinburgh University |
| **1831** | Appointed naturalist on HMS *Beagle* |
| **1832–36** | Travels in and around South America on HMS *Beagle* |
| **1842** | Writes first, 35-page draft of his evolutionary theory |
| **1858** | Alfred Russel Wallace and Darwin present joint paper to the Linnean Society in London on July 1 |
| **1859** | *On the Origin of Species by Means of Natural Selection* published on November 26 |

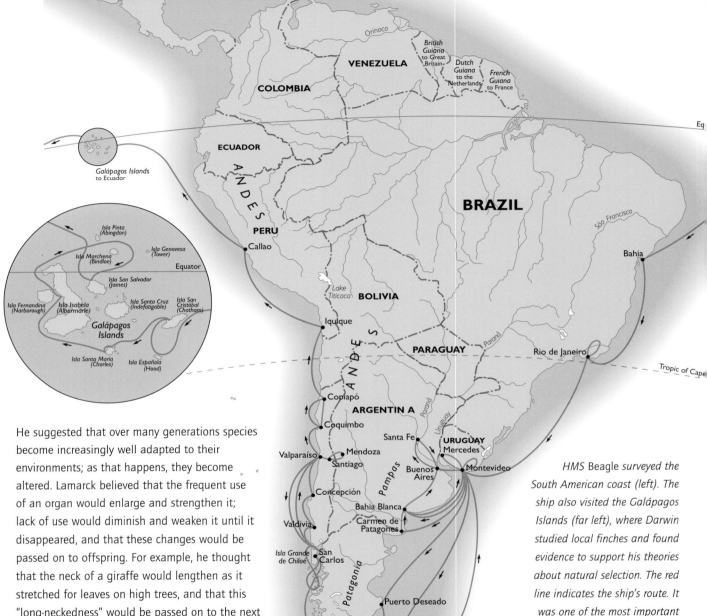

Galápagos Islands
to Ecuador

Isla Pinta
(Abingdon)
Isla Marchena
(Bindloe)
Isla Genovesa
(Tower)
Equator
Isla San Salvador
(James)
Isla Fernandina
(Narborough)
Isla Isabela
(Albermarle)
Isla Santa Cruz
(Indefatigable)
Isla San
Cristóbal
(Chatham)
Galápagos
Islands
Isla Santa María
(Charles)
Isla Española
(Hood)

VENEZUELA
COLOMBIA
Orinoco
British Guiana to Great Britain
Dutch Guiana to the Netherlands
French Guiana to France
ECUADOR
ANDES
PERU
Callao
BRAZIL
São Francisco
Bahia
Eq
Lake Titicaca
BOLIVIA
Iquique
ANDES
PARAGUAY
Paraná
Rio de Janeiro
Tropic of Cap
Copiapó
ARGENTINA
Coquimbo
Santa Fe
URUGUAY
Mercedes
Valparaíso
Mendoza
Santiago
Pampas
Buenos
Aires
Montevideo
Concepción
Bahia Blanca
Valdivia
Carmen de
Patagones
Isla Grande
de Chiloé
San
Carlos
Patagonia
Puerto Deseado
Puerto
Santa Cruz
Falkland Islands
to Great Britain
Tierra
del Fuego

He suggested that over many generations species become increasingly well adapted to their environments; as that happens, they become altered. Lamarck believed that the frequent use of an organ would enlarge and strengthen it; lack of use would diminish and weaken it until it disappeared, and that these changes would be passed on to offspring. For example, he thought that the neck of a giraffe would lengthen as it stretched for leaves on high trees, and that this "long-neckedness" would be passed on to the next generation. No instance of this "inheritance of acquired characteristics" has ever been found. Although Darwin's own theory was superficially similar to Lamarck's, it has significant differences, and was developed from the observations Darwin made on his voyage in the *Beagle*.

## THE VOYAGE OF THE *BEAGLE*

In December 1831 the *Beagle* left port. When she anchored at Saint Jago in the Cape Verde Islands, off the coast of West Africa, the rock strata there provided

*HMS* Beagle *surveyed the South American coast (left). The ship also visited the Galápagos Islands (far left), where Darwin studied local finches and found evidence to support his theories about natural selection. The red line indicates the ship's route. It was one of the most important scientific voyages of all time.*

Darwin with evidence to support the idea of slow change described in Lyell's book. He found a layer of limestone rock nearly 45 feet (14 m) above sea level that contained seashells; similar material was forming by the seashore. Clearly, either the sea was once much higher, or the land was once lower.

From here the *Beagle* crossed to Brazil, arriving in Bahía in February 1832. The town was surrounded by a

*The Toco toucan (*Ramphastos toco*) illustrated by the ornithologist John Gould (1804-1881)—one of many species seen by Darwin on his voyage.*

tropical forest. The ship sailed down the Brazilian coast, landing at Rio de Janeiro in April 1832. Darwin was transfixed by everything he saw. He collected and sent home hundreds of specimens. "You cannot imagine what a fine miserlike pleasure I enjoy," he wrote, "when examining an animal differing widely from any known genus [type]."

Next, the *Beagle* set sail for Patagonia and Tierra del Fuego. In Patagonia, Darwin found a 20-foot (6-m) high cliff embedded with huge bones, which he realized belonged to animals far bigger than any now in existence. These were the remains of giant sloths, giant armadillos, and other creatures. He saw that they resembled similar modern, much smaller, species and wondered why the giant species had become extinct.

## THE MOVING EARTH

In July 1834 Darwin explored the Chilean Andes. He found fossil seashells at 12,000 feet (3658 m), which confirmed what he had been thinking: this part of South America must once have lain beneath the sea, and later been pushed back up above sea level. The mountains would first have appeared as islands in the sea, and eventually been raised up to form mountains.

On February 20, 1835 an earthquake in Chile destroyed the city of Concepción. Darwin noticed that the level of the land had risen after the earthquake, and that a new island had emerged in the ocean close to Juan Fernández. To Darwin this was proof that land could rise up from the sea and form mountain ranges. He decided that the Earth's center must be filled with molten rock, and that "a vast lake of melted matter...is spread out beneath a mere crust of solid land."

## RETURNING HOME

In October 1836 the *Beagle* arrived back in England. Some of Darwin's geological reports had been published while he was away, and he returned to find himself recognized as a leading scientific figure. On his return to England, Darwin and his old friend and colleague John Stevens Henslow (1796–1861) began sorting the many specimens that Darwin had brought back. They also started to prepare Darwin's record of the voyage, published in 1839 as *Journal of Researches into the Geology and Natural History of the Various Countries Visited During the Voyage of HMS* Beagle *Round the World, under the Command of Capt. Fitzroy, R.N.*

## EVOLUTION BY NATURAL SELECTION

In 1837 Darwin became the secretary of the Geological Society, and in 1839 he was elected a fellow of the Royal Society. In June 1842 he wrote a draft of what would become his theory of evolution by natural selection. (Evolution is the gradual change in the characteristics of plants and animals over successive generations.) Two years later Darwin wrote a second draft. He then revised the journal, as well as writing other journals. In 1856 he started to write what he considered the most complete statement of his ideas. However, he was not yet ready to publish it.

## Alfred Russel Wallace
### 1823-1913

In 1854 the naturalist Alfred Russel Wallace explored the Malay archipelago and the East Indies (now Indonesia) where he noticed differences in the animal species of the East Indies; those in the western islands looked like species found on the mainland of Asia, and those in the eastern islands resembled Australian species. The groups are separated by a line between the islands of Borneo and Celebes (now Sulawesi) and Bali and Lombok. The line—now called Wallace's Line—follows a deep-water channel. It shows that animals on either side of the channel have been isolated from each other for a long time.

In 1855 Wallace wrote a paper called "On the Law Which Has Regulated the Introduction of New Species," admitting that he often thought about how species change.

In 1858 Wallace found himself thinking about Malthus's *Essay on Population*. In his own words, "there suddenly flashed upon me the idea of the survival of the fittest." He wrote out his idea and mailed it to Darwin. Darwin recognized that he and Wallace had both reached the same conclusion on evolution by natural selection.

### THE SAME CONCLUSION

Darwin had written about half of the book by the middle of 1858, when on June 18 he received an essay written by the Welsh naturalist Alfred Russel Wallace. Darwin realized that Wallace had reached the same conclusion as he had about the way species evolve. Both men had found that, within each species, some individuals have a characteristic (variation) that makes their survival more likely. They pass this feature on to their offspring, and gradually each generation that follows becomes more adapted to its environment. Although Darwin had formed his theory years earlier, he decided to announce his theory at the same time as Wallace, and so it was agreed that a "joint paper" would be presented to the Linnean Society in London on July 1, 1858. It attracted little interest, however.

Darwin also published a shorter account of his theory in a book called *On the Origin of Species by Means of Natural Selection, or The Preservation of Favoured Races in the Struggle for Life*. The first edition of 1,250 copies, published on November 26, 1859, sold out on the first day. Darwin admitted that his theory presented difficulties. In particular, he had no idea how variation could emerge within a species or how characters could be inherited. He suggested the environment might stimulate variation, rather in the way proposed by Lamarck.

*A contemporary etching of the city of Concepción, Chile, after the 1835 earthquake. "The world, the very emblem of all that is solid, had moved beneath our feet like a crust over a fluid," Darwin wrote.*

A cartoon in The London Sketch Book *of 1874 (far left) shows Darwin and an ape comparing their facial features in a mirror. It was a common taunt that he believed humans to be descended from monkeys, but Darwin scarcely mentions human evolution in* On the Origin of Species, *published in 1859 (above).*

The Darwinian (or Darwin-Wallace) theory proceeds in seven steps. 1. Individuals resemble their parents. 2. Individuals belonging to a species are slightly different from one another. 3. Members of each generation usually produce more offspring than are needed to replace their parents. 4. Despite this, populations tend to remain stable and it is impossible for a population to increase in size indefinitely. 5. Since populations remain stable, not all offspring can survive; therefore there must be competition to survive among the offspring. 6. Survivors will be those individuals that differ in ways that allow them to use the resources available to them more efficiently. 7. Environmental conditions change over long periods of time. These changes naturally select the variations within a species that are best suited to them; the changes also encourage new variations to emerge. Eventually the variations are so marked that a completely new species is formed, so it is natural selection, through changing environmental conditions, that causes new species to emerge.

## RELIGIOUS OBJECTIONS

Although Darwin had deliberately avoided the question of human evolution in *On the Origin of Species*, his theory of natural selection disturbed many. Religious opponents criticized it for implying that the higher powers of humans have developed naturally from characteristics already present in animals, thereby denying the belief that God has placed humans above the animals. Nevertheless Darwin continued to develop his theory, discussing human origins in *The Descent of Man, and Selection in Relation to Sex* (1871). He also wrote several other books on natural history.

## THE "THEORY OF EVOLUTION"

When scientists speak of "the theory of evolution," they mean the one put forward by Darwin and Wallace, in which natural selection is the mechanism that drives forward the evolution of species. Evolution itself is not a theory, it is a fact. Evolution is the descent of organisms from one generation to another with slight modification until they are so different from their ancestors that they make up a new species.

# CHARLES DARWIN

1820 1830 1840

## SCIENTIFIC BACKGROUND

**Before 1820**

Scottish scientist James Hutton (1726–1797) argues that the Earth is millions of years old

Darwin's grandfather, Erasmus Darwin (1731–1802), suggests that species might be transformable

French naturalist Chevalier de Lamarck (1744–1829) proposes that species can inherit characteristics acquired by the previous generation

English clergyman Thomas Malthus (1766–1834) writes an *Essay on Population* in which he maintains that a struggle for survival in populations is inevitable

**1820–40** English geologists William Buckland (1784–1836) and Adam Sedgwick (1785–1873) develop their "catastrophist" view of geological history

**1827** French mathematician Jean Baptiste Fourier (1768–1830) suggests that human activities have an effect on the Earth's climate

**1831** Darwin sets sail with Captain Robert Fitzroy on HMS *Beagle* as the expedition's unpaid naturalist

**1835** Darwin makes important discoveries about the evolution of species on the Galápagos Islands

**1837** Darwin reads Thomas Malthus's *Essay on Population*

**1839** Darwin publishes his *Journal of Researches into the Geology and Natural History of the Various Countries Visited by HMS Beagle*

**1842** Darwin writes the first draft of his theory of evolution

**1844** Robert Chambers (1802–1871) publishes anonymously his theory of the development of species in *Vestiges of Creation*

**1848–52** Welsh botanist Alfred Russel Wallace (1823–1913) collects specimens in South America

## POLITICAL AND CULTURAL BACKGROUND

**1824** German composer Ludwig van Beethoven (1770–1827) completes his *Mass in D Major*

**1826** American novelist James Fenimore Cooper (1789–1851) publishes *The Last of the Mohicans*, one of a series of novels by Cooper that take pioneer and American Indian life as their subject

**1827** *An American Dictionary of the English Language* is published after 28 years of work by American lexicographer Noah Webster (1758–1843)

**1837** American inventor Samuel Finley Breese Morse (1791–1872) patents his version of the telegraph, a machine that sends letters in code

**1837** In Britain, Queen Victoria (1819–1901) comes to the throne. She will rule for the rest of the 19th century, and until her death in 1901

**1844** American inventor Charles Goodyear (1800–60) treats rubber with sulfur under heat and pressure to make it more elastic and strong; the process, known as "vulcanizing," allows the development of the rubber tires for which he becomes famous

**1846** Famine sweeps Ireland as the potato crop fails

**1854-62** Wallace travels to the Malay archipelago and the East Indies (now Indonesia), and collects more than 125,000 specimens

**1858** Wallace reads Malthus's *Essay on Population* and forms theory of "survival of the fittest," which he sends to Darwin

**1858** Darwin and Wallace present a joint paper on their theory of natural selection to the Linnean Society in London; in 1859 Darwin publishes *On the Origin of Species by Natural Selection*

**1863** British geologist Charles Lyell (1797-1875) and British zoologist Thomas Huxley (1825-1895) publish *Antiquity of Man* and *Man's Place in Nature*

**1865** Austrian botanist Gregor Mendel (1822-1884) publishes his theory of a law of inheritance, but it does not gain much attention until 1900

**1869-1910** Darwin's cousin Francis Galton (1822-1911) develops eugenics, the idea of breeding of human beings for evolutionary improvement

**1871** Darwin's work *The Descent of Man* concludes that man evolved from apelike ancestors in Africa

**1871** A prehistoric pterodactyl skeleton is identified by the first American paleontologist, Othniel Charles Marsh (1831-1899)

**1880** French chemist Louis Pasteur (1822-1895) develops the germ theory of disease

**1887** Belgian cytologist Eduard van Beneden (1817-1910) discovers that each species has a fixed number of chromosomes

**1889** Wallace publishes *Darwinism* and receives the first Darwin Medal

**1890-96** "Lamarckism" rejected by German biologist August Weismann (1834-1919)

**After 1900**

**1900** Mendel's theory of inheritance is revived

**1902** American geneticist Walter Stanborough Sutton (1877-1916) states that chromosomes are paired and may be the carriers of heredity

---

**1850** — **1860** — **1870** — **1880** — **1890**

---

**1850** Bavarian-American entrepreneur Levi Strauss (1829-1902) introduces "bibless overalls," the forerunner of denim jeans, for miners in California

**1850** German chemist and physicist Robert Wilhelm Bunsen (1811-1899) invents the Bunsen burner

**1859** American landscape painter Frederick E. Church (1826-1900) completes *Heart of the Andes*

**1865** The American Civil War ends, President Lincoln is assassinated, and a 12-year "Era of Reconstruction" begins in the South

**1867** German social, political, and economic theorist Karl Marx (1818-1883) publishes *Das Kapital,* in which he develops the theory of the evolution of society

**1870** The Vatican Council votes that the pope is infallible when defining doctrines of faith or morals

**1877** The disputed 1876 election for the U.S. presidency is resolved when an electoral committee declares in favor of the Republican Rutherford B. Hayes (1822-1893)

**1884** American writer Mark Twain (1835-1910) publishes *The Adventures of Huckleberry Finn*. The author takes his pen-name from the phrase used by men testing depths in shallow rivers: "mark twain" means that the mark shows the river is two fathoms deep

**1886** In the United States, Coca-Cola goes on sale for the first time. Made by an Atlanta chemist, its ingredients include South American coca and African kola nuts

**1893** A four-year economic depression begins in the United States. On June 27 the Wall Street stock market collapses as share prices plummet

# LOUIS PASTEUR

## 1822–1895

*"The enchantment of science is that, everywhere and always, we can give the justification of our principles and the proof of our discoveries."*

Louis Pasteur

FRENCH CHEMIST LOUIS PASTEUR DEMONSTRATED THAT INFECTIOUS DISEASES ARE CAUSED BY MICROSCOPIC ORGANISMS CALLED GERMS. HE FOUND WAYS OF TREATING THE DISEASES, INVENTED THE PROCESS OF "PASTEURIZATION," AND DEVELOPED VACCINES FOR POTENTIALLY LETHAL DISEASES LIKE RABIES AND ANTHRAX.

Born on December 27, 1822, in Dole, France, Louis Pasteur entered the Collège Communal at Arbois in 1829. He was not a brilliant pupil, but his ambition was to become an art teacher. In 1840 he graduated in arts from the Royal College in the city of Besançon, and in 1842 he graduated in science. He entered the École Normale Supérieure in 1843, to train as a teacher, and attended lectures at the Sorbonne— part of the University of Paris—given by organic chemist Jean Baptiste André Dumas (1800-1884). Pasteur's enthusiasm for chemistry grew, so his grades improved, and he graduated as a doctor of science in 1847.

### AN EARLY HONOR

Pasteur's early scientific interests lay in the study of the structure of crystals, crystallography. He carried out detailed research into tartaric acid crystals, which he discovered have particular qualities when transmitting polarized light (light in which the wave vibrations are arranged in a single plane). This laid the foundations for stereochemistry, an important new branch of science which involved the study of the way atoms are arranged within molecules.

Pasteur presented his results to the Paris Academy of Sciences; in recognition of his achievements he was awarded the ribbon of the Légion d'Honneur in 1853. In the meantime he had met and married the daughter of the rector of the University of Strasbourg, Marie Laurent.

*As well as being a brilliant chemist, Pasteur was an accomplished artist. This pastel is of his mother.*

# THE BATTLE AGAINST INFECTION

The causes of infection were not understood in the early 19th century, so protecting against germs was nearly impossible. English nurse Florence Nightingale (1820–1910) thought that disease was caused by unpleasant fumes. She encouraged cleanliness, fresh air, and minimal furnishings in her wards, helping to reduce germs.

## Semmelweiss, Lister, and Antisepsis

The Hungarian obstetrician Ignaz Semmelweiss (1818–1865) was dismayed at the number of women dying of puerperal ("childbed") fever. He thought that students who came from the dissecting room to treat patients were carrying infection; when he told the students to wash their hands in disinfectant, the death rate among the patients dropped dramatically. This process of actually destroying germs is called antisepsis; it was developed further by the English surgeon Joseph Lister (1827–1912).

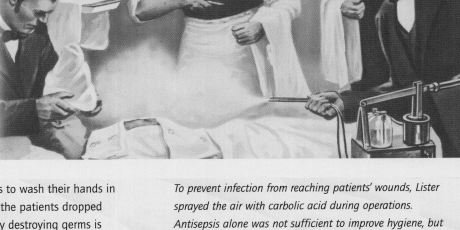

*To prevent infection from reaching patients' wounds, Lister sprayed the air with carbolic acid during operations. Antisepsis alone was not sufficient to improve hygiene, but when combined with asepsis—a germ-free environment—it proved to be a highly effective method.*

## THE SOURING OF WINE AND BEER

In 1854 Pasteur became dean and professor of chemistry at the University of Lille in France. During visits to local brewers, Pasteur became interested in fermentation, the process that changes sugars in certain foodstuffs into alcohol. Yeast is a fungus, and is used in brewing beer; at the time people believed fermentation was a chemical process, aided by the decomposition of dead yeast cells. However, Pasteur discovered that fermentation is a biological process; "live" yeast was causing fermentation by actively feeding on sugars and producing alcohol as well as carbon dioxide gas.

In 1856 a local industrialist asked Pasteur to investigate why wine and beer sometimes turn sour. Examining good and sour beer under a microscope,

## KEY DATES

| | |
|---|---|
| **1847** | Graduates as a doctor of science |
| **1856** | Awarded the Rumford medal of the Royal Society in London; investigates fermentation and putrefaction |
| **1868** | Discovers the cause of diseases in silkworms |
| **1873** | Becomes member of the French Academy of Medicine |
| **1880** | Develops a vaccine for chicken cholera |
| **1885** | Successfully inoculates first patient against rabies |
| **1887** | Becomes secretary of the French Academy of Sciences |
| **1888** | The Pasteur Institute opens in Paris |

Pasteur found that the good beer contained round yeast cells and the sour beer had rodlike yeast cells. Clearly there were two types of yeast. In the sour beer the yeast that produced alcohol was contaminated by other yeast cells to produce acetic acid (vinegar).

Pasteur found that souring could be prevented by heating beer or wine to 122°F (50°C), then sealing the container. Heating kills all the yeast, including the rodlike variety that would otherwise continue to make acetic acid while the drink was maturing.

Pasteur suspected that the yeast that made acetic acid must have entered the beer from the air. He showed that microorganisms carried in the air were responsible for the change that caused foods to ferment (change to alcohol) or to putrefy (rot and decay). Pasteurization, the process of controlled heating named after Pasteur, kills these microorganisms, and is widely used today to preserve foods. Milk is pasteurized, for example, to destroy the bacteria that form lactic acid.

## SAVING THE SILKWORMS

In the 1860s the French silk industry was devastated by a disease that killed silkworms, which are the larvae of a species of moth. In 1865 Pasteur was asked to investigate the problem. He discovered the insects were suffering from two diseases, both caused by tiny parasites. Parasites live in or on other animals or plants, known as hosts, and get their nourishment from them. Pasteur found these parasites in the debris of the mulberry leaves on which the silkworms fed, and in the bodies of infected silkworms.

Combining this discovery with his work on fermentation and putrefaction, Pasteur went on to develop the germ theory of disease. Previously people had believed that disease was spread by poisonous fumes, known as miasma, that rose up from dung heaps and decaying material. Pasteur's new theory, that disease was caused by microorganisms, gave people hope that these organisms could somehow be prevented from invading human bodies.

*Pasteur at the École Normale Supérieure, the teachers' college in Paris. The French emperor, Napoleon III (1808–1873), helped finance Pasteur's laboratory there.*

## PREVENTING CHICKEN CHOLERA

In 1878 Pasteur began working on cases of chicken cholera, a fatal disease of fowl. He isolated the germ—a microorganism called a bacterium (plural, bacteria)—and left some cultures of it while he went on vacation. Then he injected the bacterium cultures into chickens; he found that the chickens did not get the disease and that they were resistant to infection by a fresh culture.

Eventually Pasteur discovered that by leaving the culture exposed to air at about 99°F (37°C), a weak form of the disease developed. The weak culture, when injected into chickens, made them immune to chicken cholera, just as cowpox vaccine developed by English physician Edward Jenner (1749–1823) had protected people against smallpox. Pasteur also made a vaccine to protect livestock against anthrax.

## FINDING A CURE FOR RABIES

Pasteur began one of his most famous pieces of research in 1882, in which he aimed to find a way of combating rabies.

*A chocolate manufacturer's promotional advertisement praising the achievements of French science shows Pasteur with students from the University of Lille. A local industrialist is impressed by his evidence that fermentation is a biological process caused by microorganisms such as yeasts and bacteria. The caption to the picture proclaims "Pasteur discovers the law of fermentation."*

# LOUIS PASTEUR

Rabies is a disease that can be passed from infected dogs or other animals to humans through a bite; once symptoms appear, the disease is usually fatal. After experimenting with inoculations made from the saliva of animals infected with rabies (which did not work), Pasteur concluded that the germ responsible—in fact it is a virus, though they had not yet been discovered—was present in the brain and spinal column. Eventually he developed a weakened form of the infection that he could use for inoculation.

Pasteur had successfully treated animals with his vaccine, but his work was still at an experimental stage when he was unexpectedly presented with a human subject. On July 6, 1885, the mother of Joseph Meister, a nine-year-old boy who had been badly bitten by a dog with rabies, begged Pasteur to inoculate him. Since the boy would almost certainly have died within a month, Pasteur agreed to try out his vaccine. Joseph Meister was saved, and since then the Pasteur vaccine has been used to prevent the onset of rabies in many thousands of people who have been infected.

## A FITTING TRIBUTE

The success of his rabies vaccine brought Pasteur great fame. He had been made a member of the French Academy of Medicine in 1873, and in 1874 the French National Assembly awarded him a pension for life. Many people regarded Pasteur as a national hero, and the public raised money to help Pasteur in his work

In 1888 the Pasteur Institute opened in Paris. This was a private research laboratory dedicated to investigating rabies further and preventing its spread; branches followed in other parts of France and elsewhere. Louis Pasteur remained as director of the institute until he died at Saint-Cloud, near Paris, on September 28, 1895. He was buried in an elaborately tiled tomb in the Pasteur Institute.

*The French viewed Louis Pasteur as a national hero. They commemorated him and his work on this French banknote (below), which depicts Joseph Meister wrestling with the rabid dog that bit him. After a state funeral, Pasteur was laid to rest in the Pasteur Institute (bottom).*

# LOUIS PASTEUR

**Before 1820**

Dutch scientist Anton van Leeuwenhoek (1632-1723) observes "animalcules" (bacteria)

English physician Edward Jenner (1749-1823) develops a vaccine for use against smallpox

**1823** Edward Jenner dies on January 26, a month after Pasteur's birth

**1838** German physiologist Theodor Schwann (1810-1882) shows that yeast is composed of tiny living organisms; Pasteur's later work will convince scientists this is true

**1840** German anatomist Friedrich Gustav Jakob Henle (1809-1885) suggests diseases are caused by microorganisms

**1848** Hungarian obstetrician Ignaz Philipp Semmelweiss (1818-1865) introduces antiseptic methods into a Viennese maternity hospital; death rates fall dramatically

**1848** Pasteur publishes his research on stereoisomers of racemic acid

**1854** English epidemiologist John Snow (1813-1858) discovers that cholera is transmitted through contaminated water

**1856** Pasteur begins research into the process of fermentation

**1865** English surgeon Joseph Lister (1827-1912) introduces carbolic acid as an antiseptic in hospitals

**1868** Pasteur rescues the silkworm industry by discovering the causes of silkworm diseases flacherie and pébrine

**1873** Pasteur is elected to the French Academy of Medicine

**1876** German physician Robert Koch (1843-1910) identifies the bacterium that causes anthrax

**1880** Pasteur develops a vaccine against chicken cholera

**1883** Koch isolates the cause of cholera

**1885** On July 6 Pasteur successfully inoculates Joseph Meister against rabies

**After 1900**

**1906** Belgian physiologist Jules Jean Baptiste Vincent Bordet (1870-1961) discovers the bacterium that causes whooping cough

**1910** German bacteriologist Paul Ehrlich (1854-1915) uses salvarsan, the first antibacterial drug, in tests to treat syphilis

---

**1820**     **1840**     **1860**     **1880**

---

**1820** *Lamia and Other Poems* by English poet John Keats (1795-1821) is published; it includes great works such as his odes "To Autumn," "On a Grecian Urn," and "To a Nightingale"

**1824** Charles X (1757-1836) succeeds to the French throne and tries to restore the absolute power of the monarchy; he is overthrown in the revolution of July 27-29, 1830

**1844** French writer Alexandre Dumas (1802-1870) completes his novels, *The Count of Monte Cristo* and *The Three Musketeers*

**1852** American inventor Isaac Singer (1811-1875) produces a single-thread chainstitch sewing machine

**1854** The Crimean War breaks out between Russia, Britain, and France; Florence Nightingale (1820-1910) helps care for the wounded

**1865** American president Abraham Lincoln (1809-1865) is assassinated

**1874** French artist Claude Monet (1840-1926) exhibits *Impression: Sunrise*, the start of the impressionist movement in art

**1876** Scottish-born American inventor Alexander Graham Bell (1847-1922) patents his 1875 invention, the telephone

**1886** The Statue of Liberty, designed by French sculptor Auguste Bartholdi (1834-1904), is unveiled on Bedloe's Island, New York Harbor

**1903** American brothers Orville (1871-1948) and Wilbur (1867-1912) Wright make the first controlled flight in a heavier-than-air machine on December 17

# GREGOR MENDEL

## 1822–1884

*"My scientific work has brought me a great deal of satisfaction, and I am convinced that it will not be long before the whole world acknowledges [this effort]."*

Gregor Mendel

GREGOR MENDEL, AN AUSTRIAN MONK, INVESTIGATED THE WAY IN WHICH INHERITED CHARACTERISTICS ARE PASSED FROM ONE GENERATION OF PLANTS TO ANOTHER. HIS WORK LED EVENTUALLY TO THE DISCOVERY OF GENES, THE UNITS OF INHERITANCE, AND MADE POSSIBLE THE STUDY OF GENETICS.

Johann Mendel, born on July 22, 1822, later changed his first name to Gregor. The town he grew up in was then called Heizendorf, in Silesia, and was part of Austria. It is now called Hyncice and is in the Czech Republic. Mendel's parents, Anton and Rosine, were farmers, and his interest in agriculture, botany, and horticulture was first stimulated by his life on the family farm.

Mendel went to the local school, and it soon became obvious that he was very intelligent. In 1841 he enrolled at the Philosophical Institute in Olmütz (now Olomouc), hoping to become a teacher. The family could not afford to keep him there, however. A farming accident in 1838 had left Mendel's father unable to work, and several poor harvests had meant that the family had been forced to spend their savings. As the only son, Mendel would have been expected to return home and take on the farm, but he did not want to do this. Instead he joined the priesthood, which would "free him from the bitter struggle for existence," and allow him to continue studying science. In 1843 Mendel entered the Augustinian monastery in Brünn (now Brno), taking the name of Gregor.

### ENCOURAGED TO LEARN

During the 19th century there was a great growth of interest in the natural sciences. Natural sciences are those that involve the study of the physical world and everything in it, such as biology and geology. Scientists had begun to recognize the great importance of communicating their work to the public, and the public seemed keen to hear their ideas. It became common for leading citizens to set up local societies to encourage scientific research. Among those who tried to encourage an interest in science was C. F. Napp, abbot of the Brünn monastery. The monastery became a scientific

*The bustling marketplace at Brünn in 1868, the year that Gregor Mendel became abbot of the monastery there.*

institution as well as a religious one; it had a well-stocked library and provided an excellent environment for study. Abbot Napp warmed to Mendel's enthusiasm and intelligence, and welcomed him in.

Mendel continued to study science while he was preparing for the priesthood. He was ordained in 1847. For a short time in 1849 he taught mathematics and Greek in a local school, and in 1850 he took the examination for a teaching certificate, but curiously, he failed, getting low marks in biology and geology.

Abbot Napp sent the young priest to the University of Vienna where, from 1851 until 1853, Mendel studied

## KEY DATES

**1847** Ordained as a priest

**1851** Begins studying at the University of Vienna

**1854** Returns to the monastery and teaches natural science at the technical high school in Brünn

**1856** Begins breeding experiments with peas

**1865** Presents experimental results to the natural history society founded by the monks in Brünn

**1866** Publishes results of his work in "Experiments with Plant Hybrids"

**1868** Elected abbot of the monastery

*This plaque, completed in 1922, commemorates Mendel's dedication as a monk as well as his work in studying the principles of inheritance.*

a wide range of scientific subjects. In 1854 he returned to the monastery, but also began teaching natural science at the high school in Brünn. He taught there for a further 14 years.

## UNRELIABLE EXPERIMENTS

At this time Brünn was an important center of the textile industry. However, the high-quality wool that was needed for its product was not available locally, and so had to be imported from Spain. This was an expensive undertaking. People began to think about how they might improve the local sheep breeds in order to obtain better quality wool. They set up breeding programs, but these were unreliable because no one was sure how to make the next generation inherit the most desirable characteristics of the previous one. It was against this background that Mendel began his breeding experiments with peas.

In early 1865 Mendel presented his results to a natural history society founded by his fellow monks. His results were published in 1866 as an article called "Experiments with Plant Hybrids." Copies of this reached important scientific libraries in America and Europe, but it aroused no interest. Mendel sent a copy to the famous Swiss botanist Karl Wilhelm von Nägeli (1817–1891), professor of botany at the University of Munich. Nägeli read the paper but apparently failed to appreciate the implications of the work. Years later Nägeli wrote a book on genetics, but did not mention Mendel.

## MENDEL FORMULATES HIS LAWS

Mendel's study of inheritance revealed two general principles, now known as Mendel's Laws of Segregation and Independent Assortment. The Law of Segregation states that each inherited characteristic (or gene) is made up of two factors, one derived from each parent. Today these factors are called "alleles." For example, pea flowers may be purple or white, so there is an allele for purple flowers and an allele for white flowers. One allele is "dominant" and the other "recessive." In the case of pea flowers, purple is dominant and white is recessive. This can be written as capital P (dominant) and lower-case w (recessive).

When two dominant alleles are present, the characteristic associated with the dominant allele will be inherited; if a dominant allele and a recessive allele are present, the characteristic associated with the dominant allele will still be the one passed on. For example, a pea plant with Pw or PP will have purple flowers. Only if both alleles are recessive (ww) will the plant have white flowers.

Mendel's Law of Independent Assortment states that characteristics are inherited individually, not as packages. So, for example, the color of the peas (yellow or green) and their shape (smooth or wrinkled) are inherited independently of each other. So peas can be smooth and yellow, wrinkled and yellow, smooth and green, or wrinkled and green.

## A MISSED OPPORTUNITY

About the same time as Mendel was experimenting with peas, English naturalists Charles Darwin

---

### Karl Wilhelm von Nägeli
#### 1817–1891

Karl Wilhelm von Nägeli was born in Kilchberg in Switzerland and studied botany at the University of Geneva under Augustin Pyrame de Candolle (1778–1841), who introduced the term "taxonomy" to plant classification. Aged only 25 Nägeli wrote a paper on pollen formation, describing cell division and "transitory cytoblasts;" these were later recognized as chromosomes. He was professor at the University of Munich, Germany, from 1858. Despite his important contributions to botany, Nägeli clung to old ideas, rejecting the view that environmental influences could cause variations in species. His belief that evolution occurred in jumps probably blinded him to the importance of the paper that Mendel sent him in 1866.

---

(1809–1882) and Alfred Russel Wallace (1823–1913) were (separately) working out the theory of evolution by natural selection. They had both noticed that all individuals vary slightly. They had also seen that, within a particular habitat (the natural home of an animal or plant), some variations give the individuals that possessed them an advantage when it comes to reproduction. The individuals that possess these advantages will survive in greater numbers than those that do not, and will pass them on to their offspring, so eventually individuals with these advantages become predominant. This is "natural selection," and Darwin and Wallace showed it is what drives the way animals and plants develop over time, or "evolve." However, neither Darwin nor Wallace knew how variation in species occurred; it was Mendel's work on heredity that helped biologists understand how characteristics could be passed on.

Mendel's results, published a few years after Darwin's *On the Origin of Species* (1859), could have lent support to Darwin's theory of natural selection. However, although a copy of Mendel's paper, written in German, was sent to Darwin, he never read it.

# GREGOR MENDEL

## HEAD OF THE MONASTERY

In 1868 Mendel was elected abbot, or head, of the monastery. Although he remained interested in botany, meteorology, and bee-keeping, the day-to-day running of the monastery left him little time for research or teaching. He died at Brünn on January 6, 1884.

## REDISCOVERING MENDEL'S WORK

In 1900 Mendel's work was rediscovered. Three scientists who were working independently on heredity (the transmission of characteristics from one generation to another)—Dutch botanist Hugo de Vries (1848–1935), German botanist Karl Erich Correns (1864–1933), and Austrian botanist Erich Tschermak von Seysenegg (1872–1962)—all came across copies of Mendel's paper on peas and drew attention to it. Their own work seemed to confirm Mendel's belief that characteristics are inherited in a ratio of 3:1. British scientist William Bateson (1861–1926) translated the paper into English, and through his own studies of the inheritance of comb shape in fowl, showed that Mendelian ratios are found in animal crosses as well as

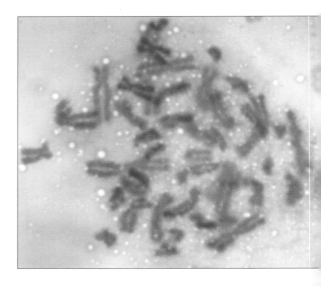

*These human chromosomes, magnified 500 times, are undergoing cell division. Chromosomes carry the units of inheritance called genes.*

plants. It was Bateson who introduced the term "genetics" to describe the science of heredity that Mendel had founded.

## CHROMOSOMES AND GENES

By the end of the 19th century some scientists believed that heredity had its basis inside the nucleus of cells. In 1879 the German biologist Walther Flemming (1843–1905) had found that tiny rod-shaped structures—later called chromosomes—were present in dividing cells; these were identified as what passed on particular characteristics (what Mendel called "heritable factors") to offspring.

In the early 1900s the American biologist and geneticist Thomas Hunt Morgan (1866–1945) begin studying the fruit fly (*Drosophila melanogaster*). By 1911 Morgan was convinced that Mendel's heritable factors were actually physical units, which were given the name "genes." Morgan showed that genes were located at particular positions along the rodlike chromosomes, like beads on a necklace. Morgan and his colleagues produced a chromosome "map," showing the position of five genes. Nowadays scientists have mapped hundreds of genes.

Scientists now know that genes that are on the same chromosome are more likely to be inherited together than genes that are on different chromosomes, and that the closer they are to each other on the chromosome the more likely they are to be inherited together. This association, known as "linkage," was also discovered by Morgan.

*Morgan's breeding experiments with fruit flies (left) confirmed Mendel's theory of "heritable factors," and proved these were physical units, or genes.*

# GREGOR MENDEL

**SCIENTIFIC BACKGROUND**

**Before 1840**

English naturalist Charles Darwin (1809–1882) notes that different species of Galápagos Island finches seem to have developed from a single mainland-based ancestor

Animal and plant cells are described by German physiologist Theodor Schwann (1810–1882) and German botanist Matthias Schleiden (1804–1881)

**1849** American naturalist Luther Burbank (1849–1926) begins developing new plant varieties, including the Burbank potato, the Shasta daisy, and different varieties of plums and berries

**1851** German botanist Wilhelm Hofmeister (1824–1877) discovers the "alternation of generations"; that generations of mosses and ferns are alternately sexual and nonsexual

**1856** Mendel begins his experimentation using pea plants

**1858** Charles Darwin and Welsh naturalist Alfred Wallace (1823–1913) put forward their theory of natural selection in a joint paper to the Linnean Society in London

**1859** Darwin publishes his great work, *On the Origin of Species By Means of Natural Selection*

**1865** French botanist Charles Naudin (1815–1899) describes his "theory of disjunction," which correctly concludes that inheritance is not a blending process

**1866** Mendel publishes the results of his experiments in "Experiments with Plant Hybrids"

**1868** Darwin publishes *The Variation of Animals and Plants Under Domestication*, expanding on his theory of natural selection

**1875** German botanist Eduard Strasburger (1844–1912) publishes *Cell Formation and Cell Division*, in which he lays down the basic principles of the study of plant cells

**After 1880**

**1900** Dutch botanist Hugo de Vries (1848–1935) is among several botanists who rediscover Mendel's work on heredity

**1902** English geneticist William Bateson (1861–1926) writes a defence of Mendel's work and later coins the term "genetics"

**1911** American biologist Thomas Hunt Morgan (1866–1945) identifies heritable factors as genes

---

**1840**   **1850**   **1860**   **1870**

---

**POLITICAL AND CULTURAL BACKGROUND**

**1845** The failure of the potato crop on which so many European people are dependent leads to the death of 2.5 million people there from famine; Ireland is particularly hard hit

**1848** As revolution sweeps France, King Louis-Philippe (1773–1850) is forced to abdicate; he flees to Britain, calling himself "Mr Smith"

**1851** The Great Exhibition is held in London's newly built Crystal Palace; it is the first world trade fair

**1852** American writer Harriet Beecher Stowe (1811–1896) completes her antislavery novel, *Uncle Tom's Cabin*, which sells 300,000 copies in the United States alone

**1860** Construction begins on the world's first underground railroad system, in London

**1863** The American Civil War turns in favor of Union forces when they win victories at Gettysburg, Pennsylvania, and Vicksburg, Michigan, preventing an invasion of the North and gaining control of the Mississippi River

**1870** United States oil magnate John Davison Rockefeller (1839–1937) founds the Standard Oil Company with his brother William (1841–1922)

**1877** *Black Beauty*, by English novelist Anna Sewell (1820–1878), will become a worldwide bestselling book

# ALEXANDER FLEMING

## 1881–1955

*"People have called it a miracle. For once in my life as a scientist, I agree. It is a miracle, and it will save lives by thousands."*

Alexander Fleming

UNTIL THE ACCIDENTAL DISCOVERY OF PENICILLIN BY SCOTTISH BACTERIOLOGIST ALEXANDER FLEMING, PEOPLE OFTEN DIED FROM INFECTIOUS DISEASES OR FROM INFECTION FOLLOWING SURGERY. FLEMING'S WORK LED TO THE DEVELOPMENT OF BACTERIA-DESTROYING CHEMICALS CALLED ANTIBIOTICS.

Born in Lochfield, Scotland, on August 6, 1881, Alexander Fleming attended Kilmarnock Academy, but in 1894 his father died and he went to live in London. He went on to study medicine and graduated in 1906. He spent the rest of his career at St. Mary's Hospital, part of London University.

### BACTERIOLOGY AND IMMUNIZATION

Fleming began as a surgeon, but soon switched to bacteriology—the study of tiny bacteria present in water, soil, and the bodies of plants and animals. Some are harmless, or even beneficial, but others produce toxins (poisons) that cause infection and disease. German physician Robert Koch (1843–1910) and French chemist Louis Pasteur (1822–1895) had already isolated some disease-causing bacteria and developed vaccines to provide immunization against them.

Immunization increases resistance to infection by stimulating the production of antibodies, part of the body's defense system. Antibodies are proteins made by white blood cells in response to the foreign molecules (antigens) produced by disease-causing bacteria; they make the antigens harmless. Somebody who has recovered from an infectious disease such as measles will have natural immunity against future attacks because the antibodies persist in the blood stream.

Immunization against a specific disease can be induced by introducing antibodies from an infected person or animal into the blood stream to stimulate the development of the antibodies to fight it. This is known as vaccination or inoculation, and was first used against smallpox in the 18th century. Immunization was a powerful tool in preventing the spread of diseases. But bacteriologists had yet to find a way to destroy bacteria causing infection within the body. Several antibacterial agents (chemicals that kill bacteria) had been found by the early 20th century, but all of them had harmful effects on human tissue.

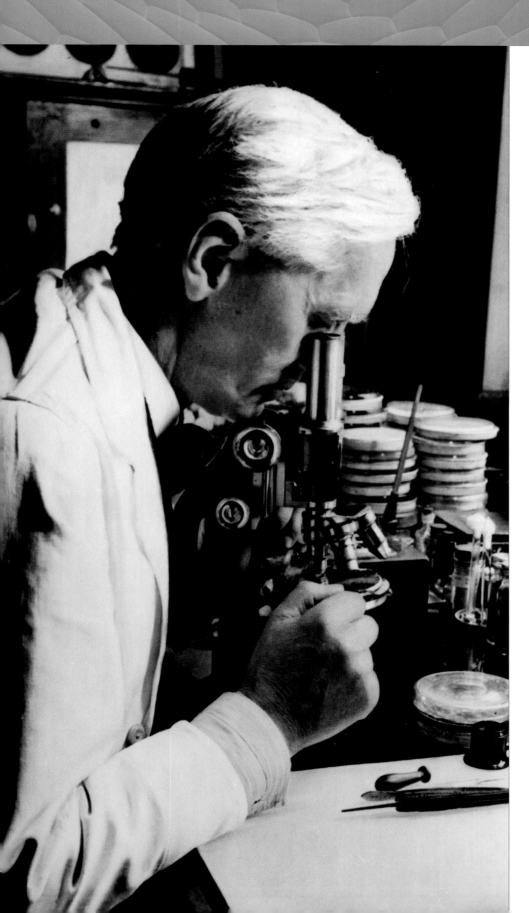

## KEY DATES

**1894** Fleming's father dies; Alexander moves to London to live with one of his brothers, a doctor

**1900** Enlists in the army

**1902** Begins studies at St. Mary's Hospital Medical School, part of London University

**1906** Graduates from medical school

**1914–18** Serves in the Royal Army Medical Corps

**1920** Appointed director of the Department of Systematic Bacteriology and assistant director of the Inoculation Department at St. Mary's

**1922** Discovers lysozyme, a protein that kills bacteria

**1928** Becomes professor of bacteriology at St. Mary's and lecturer at the Royal College of Surgeons; discovers penicillin

**1929** Publishes results of work with Penicillium mold

**1944** Is knighted to become Sir Alexander Fleming

**1945** Shares the Nobel Prize for physiology or medicine with Ernst Chain (1906–1979) and Howard Florey (1898–1968)

*Sir Alexander Fleming photographed studying bacteria cultures through a microscope in his laboratory at St. Mary's Hospital in London.*

## Ernst Boris Chain
### 1906–1979

British biochemist Ernst Chain was born in Berlin, Germany. He graduated in chemistry and physiology from the Friedrich Wilhelm Institute, and then worked at the Institute of Pathology, Charité Hospital, Berlin from 1930 to 1933. The anti-Jewish policies of Germany's Adolf Hitler (1889–1945) forced him to flee to England, where he worked at Cambridge University before joining Florey at Oxford University in 1935. They isolated penicillin and demonstrated its unique antibacterial properties.

After the war, having shared the 1945 Nobel Prize for physiology or medicine with Florey and Fleming, Chain became director of the International Research Center for Chemical Microbiology in Rome. In 1954 he helped pharmaceutical company the Beecham Group to develop a range of semi-synthetic penicillins.

In 1961 Chain returned to England to become professor of biochemistry at Imperial College, University of London. He held various posts there until 1979. He died in Ireland the same year.

### SOME IMPORTANT DISCOVERIES

In 1914 Europe was plunged into war. Fleming served in the army medical corps throughout World War I. Many soldiers died from flesh wounds because doctors were unable to prevent bacterial infection from causing major infections such as septicemia (blood poisoning). Fleming was determined to find a substance that would destroy harmful bacteria. After the war he investigated various secretions of the body for their effects on bacteria. In 1922 he discovered lysozyme, an enzyme (protein molecule) present in tears and saliva. Fleming showed that lysozome has some bacteria-destroying power.

In 1928 Fleming, now professor of bacteriology at St. Mary's, made his most famous discovery. Some cultures he had left uncovered for a few days contained some specks of green mold on the agar gel. This was fairly common, but he also noticed that there was a bacteria-free circle around each speck of mold: the bacteria in the area around the mold had been killed.

Fleming identified the mold as the fungus *Penicillium notatum*. When he exposed a number of disease-causing bacteria to the mold he found that the mold killed some of them. Fleming decided that the mold must be giving off a substance that was fatal to the bacteria, and he called this "penicillin." However, he failed to isolate the penicillin from the mold. He reported his findings to the *British Journal of Experimental Pathology* (1929), but they aroused little interest. Fortunately, he kept a sample of his mold.

### DRUGS FROM DYES

Meanwhile, German biochemist Gerhard Domagk (1895–1964) made a breakthrough. He was interested in the work of Paul Ehrlich (1854–1915), who had pioneered chemotherapy using dyes. Chemotherapy is the use of toxic chemicals to attack the causes of disease. Domagk tested various dyes for their effectiveness against infections. In 1932 he found that a derivative of a dye called Prontosil red cured mice infected with streptococcal bacteria—responsible for diseases such as scarlet fever. The active chemical in the drug was called sulfanilamide. Two more chemicals, produced in 1938 and 1940, proved effective against pneumonia, and a third in 1941 was successful in treating the brain infection meningitis. Known as sulfa drugs, they saved many lives in their early years of use.

### A VALUABLE POWDER

In 1935 pathologist Howard Florey (1898–1968) and biochemist Ernst Chain began researching antibacterial substances to control wound infection. In 1938, after Chain came across Fleming's observations of the behavior of the *Penicillium notatum* mold, he and Florey decided to try to isolate the substance. This proved to be a long and difficult business, but eventually they extracted some penicillin in the form of a yellow

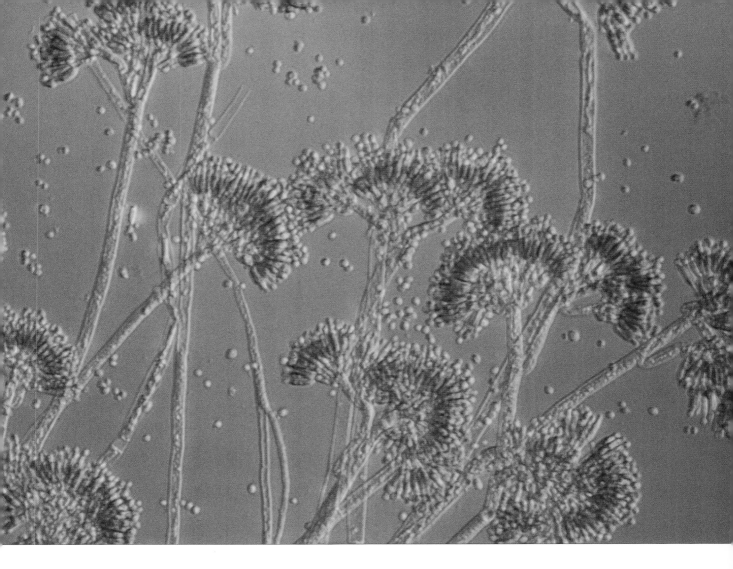

powder. They found that a solution of one part of the yellow powder in a million parts of a solvent prevented the growth of lethal bacteria in mice.

Now they decided to try the substance on a human subject. Unfortunately, their first patient, although recovering, died because they ran out of penicillin. But penicillin had proved its effectiveness. The problem was maintaining a sufficient supply, but production speeded up after the United States entered World War II in 1941.

## CONTINUING THE WORK

After his discovery of penicillin, Fleming had gone on to do other important work, identifying the organisms that infect wounds and developing new techniques for staining bacteria. He studied the effects of various disinfectants on different bacterial species and showed how streptococcal cross-infections can occur in hospitals.

*The* Penicillium *mold that produces the drug penicillin. It is shown here magnified 400 times.*

In the 1960s Chain went on to discover penicillinase, an enzyme that some bacteria can learn to synthesize, which makes them resistant to penicillin. Alexander Fleming and Howard Florey were knighted for the part they had played in developing penicillin, and in 1945 Alexander Fleming, Howard Florey, and Ernst Chain shared the Nobel Prize for physiology or medicine.

Fleming retired in 1954. Although Florey and Chain had been responsible for penicillin's transformation into a usable drug, it was Fleming who had become identified in the public mind with its creation, resulting in the "Fleming myth," as he himself called it. After his death on March 11, 1955, he was buried in St. Paul's Cathedral, London.

## SCIENTIFIC BACKGROUND

**Before 1920**

The German bacteriologist Robert Koch (1843–1910) isolates several bacteria, including those for the lung disease tuberculosis and the acute infection of the intestines, cholera

The German bacteriologists Paul Ehrlich (1854–1915) and Emil von Behring (1854–1917), and the Japanese bacteriologist Shibasaburo Kitasato (1856–1931) develop an antitoxin against diphtheria, a disease that causes fever and breathing difficulties; Ehrlich later develops salvarsan (a compound of the poison arsenic) to treat syphilis

**1922** Fleming discovers that lysozyme, a protein molecule in bodily fluids, helps the human body to limit bacterial infection

**1922** The Ehrlich–Behring–Kitasato antitoxin has brought annual deaths from diphtheria down from 43.3 per 100,000 members of the population in 1900 to 14.6 per 100,000

**1928** Fleming observes mold of the fungus *Penicillium notatum* killing bacteria; he calls this antibacterial substance penicillin, but does not isolate it

**1929** Fleming publishes his findings about *Penicillium* mold

**1932** The German biochemist Gerhard Domagk (1895–1964) finds the first "sulfa drug," a sulfonamide compound that can be used to treat bacterial infections

**1920**     **1925**     **1930**

## POLITICAL AND CULTURAL BACKGROUND

**1922** The 26 counties of southern Ireland sign a treaty with Britain to become the Irish Free State; the remaining six counties of Northern Ireland remain part of the United Kingdom

**1925** The SS (*Schutzstaffel*) is founded as a personal bodyguard for German leader Adolf Hitler (1889–1945); its members will become ruthless enforcers of the Nazi regime

**1927** In the United States *The Jazz Singer*, starring Al Jolson (1886–1950), plays to amazed audiences; it is the first "talkie," featuring speech and music synchronized to the action

**1930** The first association football (soccer) World Cup is held in Uruguay; the final, between Uruguay and Argentina, is won 4–2 by the home team

**1932** Franklin Delano Roosevelt (1882–1945) is elected to the American presidency on his promise of a "New Deal" to bring the country out of economic recession

**1933** In Germany the Nazis and their allies gain the power to rule without reference to the Reichstag (the Parliament); the Nazis go on to launch a campaign of persecution against German Jews

**1935** In Oxford, England, Australian-born Howard Florey (1898–1968) and German-born Ernst Chain (1906–1979) begin work into antibacterial substances

**1938** Domagk finds a sulfa drug that is effective against pneumonia

**1939** Florey and Chain isolate and purify a small sample of penicillin

**1939** The French-born American bacteriologist René Jules Dubos (1901–1982) isolates the antibacterial substance tyrothricin from soil bacteria, but it is too toxic to be taken internally by humans

**1941** Pharmaceutical companies begin to produce penicillin for Allied troops

**1941** Domagk finds a sulfa drug that is effective in some cases of meningitis

**1943** In the United States the Russian-born biologist Selman Waksman (1888–1973), who has coined the term "antibiotic" for antibacterial substances such as penicillin, isolates streptomycin, the first antibiotic to be effective against tuberculosis

**1945** Fleming, Florey, and Chain share the Nobel Prize for physiology or medicine

**1946** Fleming reports that insufficient doses of penicillin lead to resistant strains of bacteria

**1948** Researchers use penicillin to prevent bacterial contamination of experimental virus cultures

**1949** Waksman isolates neomycin, which can be used to treat skin, eye, and bowel infections

**1952** Waksman wins the Nobel Prize for physiology or medicine for his discovery of streptomycin

**After 1955**

**1988** American chemists Gertrude Elion (1918–1999) and George Hitchings (1905–1998) and Scottish pharmacologist James Black (1924– ) win the Nobel Prize for physiology or medicine for their work designing new drug treatments. Elion and Hitchings have developed a range of "antimetabolites," including acyclovir, one of the first drugs to be used to treat a virus, herpes; while Black has produced "beta-blockers" for use in treating heart disease

## 1935  1940  1945  1950  1955

**1936** At the Berlin Olympics in Germany, intended by Hitler to be a showcase of white Aryan supremacy, black American athlete Jesse Owens (1913–1980) wins four gold medals

**1937** The tragic last moments of the airship *Hindenburg*, which crashes in New Jersey killing 36 people, are dramatically conveyed to the public by a news reporter

**1939** World War II (1939–45) begins in Europe as German forces invade Poland on September 1; Britain and France declare war on Germany two days later

**1943** The Clinton Engineer Works, later known as Oak Ridge, is built near Knoxville, Tennessee; it is the world's first operational nuclear reactor

**1944** In the Soviet Union the siege of Leningrad by German troops finally ends in January; it has lasted 900 days and 900,000 of the city's 3 million inhabitants have died

**1948** The Jewish state of Israel is proclaimed, with Chaim Weizmann (1874–1952) as president and David Ben-Gurion (1886–1973) as premier

**1949** American boxer Joe Louis (1914–1981) retires undefeated after 12 years as world heavyweight boxing champion

**1950** The Korean War begins as the Soviet-backed North Koreans launch an attack on the South. United Nations troops, dominated by American forces, try to repel the invasion; an armistice is eventually signed on July 27, 1953

**1954** The U.S. Supreme Court rules that educating black and white people separately is unconstitutional; a growing civil rights movement is headed by Baptist minister Martin Luther King Jr. (1929–1968)

# LOUIS, MARY, AND RICHARD LEAKEY

1903–1972, 1913–1996, 1944–

*"[Mary's] commitment to detail and perfection made my father's career... She was much more organized and structured.... He was much more excitable, a magician."*

Richard Leakey

MUCH OF WHAT WE KNOW ABOUT OUR EARLIEST ANCESTORS COMES FROM THE LEAKEYS' WORK. THEIR DISCOVERIES IN AFRICA SUGGESTED STRONGLY THAT HUMAN EVOLUTION HAD BEGUN THERE, NOT IN ASIA AS WAS ORIGINALLY THOUGHT. THEY ALSO SHOWED THAT HUMANS HAD EXISTED FOR MUCH LONGER THAN PREVIOUSLY BELIEVED.

Louis Seymour Bazett Leakey was born on August 7, 1903, in Kabete, Kenya. In 1922 he went to Cambridge University to study French and Kikuyu, but in 1924 changed to studying archeology and anthropology. Anthropology is the study of humans and their culture. Louis graduated in 1926, and returned to Africa, where he met his first wife, Frida Avern. In 1930 Louis was awarded a Ph.D. from Cambridge University.

## AN IMPORTANT MEETING
Leakey carried out some work in the Olduvai Gorge in Tanzania before returning to England in 1933. There he met Mary Nicol. Mary was born in London on February 6, 1913. Louis and Mary shared a fascination with archeology and anthropology and soon became very close. Eventually Louis's wife Frida filed for divorce, and in 1936 Louis and Mary married. They were to have three sons, Jonathan, Richard, and Philip.

In 1937 Louis and Mary returned to Olduvai Gorge. Louis studied the Kikuyu people and Mary excavated a late Stone Age site near Lake Nakuru, Kenya. There she found primitive tools, burial mounds, and traces of dwellings. Their explorations in the Rift Valley yielded stone tools in the form of handaxes and hammerstones.

## ANCESTORS OF HUMANS
The tools had been made by a hominid called *Homo erectus* ("upright man"). Hominids are primates (a type of mammal) of which only one species—humans—exists today. Hominids include the direct ancestors of modern humans. At this time, most people believed that *Homo erectus* was the earliest hominid. The first *Homo erectus* fossil was found in Java, Asia, by Eugene Dubois (1858–1940) in 1891. It was dated to about 500,000 years ago. Most paleontologists (paleontology is the study of fossil remains) believed that Asia was where

the human line split from the other apes. Then, in 1924, South African anatomist Raymond Dart (1893–1988) found a hominid skull that he named *Australopithecus africanus*. Dart's assertion that this was a stage between apes and humans provoked controversy, but later discoveries of australopithecines (a genus of hominids that lived between 4.4 million and 1 million years ago) proved that his finding was correct.

## MORE FINDS

In 1959 in Olduvai Gorge Mary discovered the skull of another human ancestor. Louis allocated it to a new genus, *Zinjanthropus*, but it is now called *Australopithecus boisei*. The following year two *Homo* teeth were discovered at Olduvai Gorge, and in 1964

## KEY DATES

| | |
|---|---|
| **1937–39** | Louis studies the customs of the Kikuyu people |
| **1947** | Mary finds fossils of *Proconsul* at Rusinga Island |
| **1959** | Mary discovers *Zinjanthropus* at Olduvai on July 17 |
| **1960** | Mary and son Jonathan discover fossils of *Homo habilis*; Leakeys find *H. erectus* |
| **1963** | Richard Leakey discovers an australopithecine jaw |
| **1978** | Mary discovers hominid footprints at Laetoli |
| **1984** | Richard discovers "Turkana Boy" at Koobi Fora |
| **1995** | Richard's wife Meave discovers *Australopithecus anamensis* |

the Leakeys discovered the remains of the skull and hand bones of a species Louis classified as *Homo habilis*. The remains were 1.7 million years old, so this was clearly a species that had existed between the australopithecines and *Homo erectus*.

## A FINE LEGACY

Louis's contribution to our understanding of human ancestry was probably greater than that of any other individual. He inspired others, and he wrote numerous scientific papers and several popular books. These included *Stone Age Africa: An Outline of Prehistory in Africa* (1936), as well as his autobiography.

## FOOTPRINTS FROM LONG AGO

In 1974 American paleoanthropologist Donald Johanson (1943– ) discovered a partial female skeleton of *Australopithecus afarensis* in Ethiopia. This was a type of gracile australopithecine (the line of australopithecines from which humans may have

*Louis Leakey (right) examines the skull of* Australopithecus boisei, *discovered by Mary in 1959 and believed to be about 1.8 million years old. Mary is shown at Olduvai Gorge (below).*

evolved) that lived from 3.9 to 3.0 million years ago. Believed to be about 3.5 million years old, the fossil was nicknamed "Lucy."

In 1978, at Laetoli, near Olduvai, Mary Leakey and her team made an exciting discovery—two trails of hominid footprints. Two individuals had walked side by side through volcanic ash nearly 3.7 million years ago, leaving a trail that was immediately covered by fresh deposits. A third, perhaps a child, had trodden in the footsteps of the larger individual. The footprints are probably those of *Australopithecus afarensis*, the species that Lucy belonged to. The footprints provided firm evidence that early hominids walked on two legs.

Mary left Laetoli soon after the discovery to tour, lecture, and raise funds. Her autobiography, *Disclosing the Past*, was published in 1984.

## RICHARD LEAKEY (1944– )

Richard Erskine Frere Leakey was born at Nairobi on December 19, 1944. At first he did not want to become a paleontologist, and so he became a safari guide, combining this with capturing wild animals and supplying skeletons to museums. In 1963, while leading an expedition in the area around

# THE USE OF TOOLS

The story of early human development can be traced through the study of the tools used by the first hominids. Mary Leakey contributed much to the picture with her painstaking analysis of the large collections of pebble stone tools that the Leakeys discovered in the lowest layers of the Olduvai Gorge, dating to between 1.9 and 1.5 million years ago. The tools had been made by using a smooth pebble as a hammer in order to chip small, sharp-edged flakes off another rock or pebble. These flakes could be used for cutting and scraping. The tools Mary Leakey found at Olduvai were made by early species of *Homo*. They were used to cut meat off animals that were already dead and to scrape flesh from animal hides.

About 1.4 million years ago larger, more highly fashioned handaxes and cleavers began to be made. They are called Acheulean (after St. Acheul, France, where they were first identified), and were made by *Homo erectus*, who began to migrate from Africa about 1 million years ago. Acheulean tools, found in Africa, the Near East, and Europe, were in use until about 200,000 years ago.

*The first tools utilized by human beings were made by using a hammerstone to chip sharp flakes off other pebbles. The pebble tool above left, from Olduvai Gorge, is nearly 2 million years old. It would have been used for chopping and scraping. At right is a late Acheulean handax that dates from approximately 250,000 years ago.*

Lake Natron, in Tanzania, Richard discovered an australopithecine jaw. This discovery inspired him to become a paleontologist. In 1965 he went to London and caught up on two years of missed high school in six months, after which he returned to Africa.

## MORE HUMAN ANCESTORS REVEALED

In 1968 Richard became director of the National Museum of Kenya and began excavating at Koobi Fora on Lake Turkana (then called Lake Rudolf), which has become one of the richest repositories of early hominid fossils and stone tools in Africa. He and his team found about 400 fossil bones from about 230 individual hominids, including part of an early *Homo* skull, discovered in 1972, which may be 2 million years old. Another sensational find was "Turkana Boy," the most complete skeleton of an early hominid yet known. The fossil, discovered in 1984, is about 1.5 million years old and is classed as *Homo ergaster*.

In 1970 Richard married Meave Epps, also a paleontologist and primatologist. In 1992 she found a previously unknown species, *Australopithecus anamensis*. This was followed in 2001 by the discovery of a fossil between 3.5–3.2 million years old west of Lake Turkana. Named *Kenyanthropus platyops*, its cheek bones and flat face resembled those of a modern human.

During the 1980s Richard began to give most of his time to wildlife conservation, directing the Kenya Wildlife Service from 1989–94. In 1995 he founded a political party called Safina, and in 1998 was elected to the Kenyan Parliament. His daughter Louise (1972– ) manages her own paleontological excavations.

# LOUIS, MARY, AND RICHARD LEAKEY

## SCIENTIFIC BACKGROUND

**Before 1945**

Fossil remains of Neanderthal Man (*Homo neanderthalis*) are found in Europe

Fossils found in Asia of the earlier "Java Man" or "Peking Man" (*Homo erectus*) are taken as evidence that humans began in Asia

Fossil remains of "Piltdown Man," found in England, are hailed as the "missing link," the earliest known human remains, later to be revealed as a fake

In Botswana Australian-born South African anatomist Raymond Dart (1893–1988) finds the "Tuang Child," *Australopithecus africanus*, which he is convinced is an early human ancestor; other scientists dismiss his claim

**1947** In South Africa, the Scots-born paleontologist Robert Broom (1866–1951) finds a nearly complete skull of *Australopithecus africanus*

**1947** Mary Leakey finds fossils of apes from the extinct genus *Proconsul* at Rusinga Island in Kenya's Lake Victoria

**1948** The Leakeys piece together the skull of a *Proconsul africanus*, the first complete *Proconsul* skull

**1953** The Piltdown skull is revealed as a forgery

**1953** Louis Leakey publishes a book on human origins, *Adam's Ancestors*

**1959** At Olduvai Gorge in Tanganyika (now Tanzania) Mary Leakey discovers "Nutcracker Man" (now known as *Australopithecus boisei*)

## 1945 — 1950 — 1955

## POLITICAL AND CULTURAL BACKGROUND

**1946** In the wake of Japan's defeat in World War II (1939–45), French forces return to Southeast Asia to reclaim French colonies in Indochina. They are attacked by nationalist Vietnamese led by the Communist Ho Chi-Minh (1890–1969)

**1947** India becomes an independent nation within the British Commonwealth

**1952** A state of emergency is declared in Kenya as Kikuyu-speaking Mau Mau rebels mount an armed campaign to drive white settlers from the country

**1954** In the United States the legal case of Brown versus the Board of Education of Topeka results in a ruling by the U.S. Supreme Court that racial segregation (separating black and white pupils) in schools is unconstitutional

**1955** The American film actor James Dean (1931–1955), who has gained international popularity after the release of *East of Eden* and *Rebel Without a Cause*, dies in a car crash

**1956** A brutal military intervention by Soviet and other Warsaw Pact forces puts down an anti-Communist uprising in Hungary

**1959** After two years of guerrilla warfare, the rebel troops of Fidel Castro (1927– ) take control in Cuba

**1960** In the Olduvai Gorge, the Leakeys find a tooth of *Homo erectus* and a tooth later identified as that of *Homo habilis*

**1961** Louis Leakey founds Kenya's National Museum Center for Prehistory and Paleontology

**1964** In the Olduvai Gorge, the Leakeys find skull and hand bones of *Homo habilis*, as well as remains of *Homo erectus*

**1965** Richard Leakey goes to England to complete high school requirements, which he does in 6 months; despite passing entrance exams to university he returns to Kenya

**1971** The English animal behaviorist Jane Goodall (1934– ) publishes *In the Shadow of Man*, based on her observations of chimpanzees on the shores of Lake Tanganyika

**1972** Richard Leakey finds a fossil of *Homo habilis* at Koobi Fora on the shores of Lake Turkana in northwestern Kenya

**1974** In Ethiopia, paleoanthropologist Donald Johanson (1943– ) discovers "Lucy," *Australopithecus afarensis*

**1975** Richard Leakey's team at Koobi Fora finds fossils of *Homo erectus*

**1976** Richard Leakey's team at Koobi Fora discovers a new hominid species, *Australopithecus ethiopicus*

**1978** In Tanzania, Mary Leakey's team discovers footprints of hominid *Australopithecus afarensis*, proving that the species walked on two legs

**1984** Richard Leakey and his team discover "Turkana Boy" (*Homo ergaster*) at Koobi Fora

**After 1985**

**1987** Geneticists argue on the basis of DNA studies that all modern humans are descended from one woman who lived, probably in Africa, about 200,000 years ago

**1994** Paleontologists working in Ethiopia discover *Ardipithecus ramidus*, the oldest-known direct ancestor of humans

**2002** Skull of fossil ape *Sahelanthropus tchadensis* discovered in Chad

---

## 1960  1965  1970  1975  1980

---

**1963** Kenya becomes an independent nation within the British Commonwealth, with Jomo Kenyatta (1893–1978), formerly imprisoned as a suspected Mau Mau leader, as its first prime minister

**1963** The epic film *Cleopatra*, starring English-born American actress Elizabeth Taylor (1932– ) and Welsh actor Richard Burton (1925–1984), is the most expensive ever made

**1965** The United States launches a major bombing campaign against North Vietnam, committing U.S. ground forces to fight alongside the anti-Communist South Vietnamese army

**1968** In the Mexico Olympics American high-jumper Dick Fosbury (1947– ) introduces the head-first backward twist over the crossbar that becomes known as the "Fosbury flop"

**1973** The United States withdraws from Vietnam and a Communist government later takes over the country

**1974** Richard Nixon (1913–1994) resigns as President of the United States; evidence has emerged that he has used his office to cover up Republican involvement in a break-in at Democratic party offices at the Watergate Hotel, Washington D.C.

**1975** *Jaws*, a film by American filmmaker Steven Spielberg (1947– ) about a man-eating shark, is the commercial hit of the year

**1980** A former member of the Beatles pop group, English singer John Lennon (1940–1980), is shot dead in New York

# MELVIN CALVIN

## 1911–1997

*"He was a very, very curious man.
He loved to find things out..."*

Elin Sowle, Calvin's daughter

THE DETAILS OF PHOTOSYNTHESIS, THE PROCESS BY WHICH GREEN PLANTS (AND SOME BACTERIA) UTILIZE THE ENERGY OF SUNLIGHT TO MAKE SUGAR MOLECULES AND OXYGEN FROM WATER AND CARBON DIOXIDE, WAS EXPLAINED BY MELVIN CALVIN. ANIMALS CANNOT MAKE FOOD THIS WAY. THEY GET ENERGY DIRECTLY OR INDIRECTLY FROM PLANTS, SO PHOTOSYNTHESIS IS VITAL TO ALL LIFE.

Melvin Calvin, the son of Russian parents who had emigrated to the United States, was born in St. Paul, Minnesota, on April 8, 1911. He graduated in chemistry in 1931, and received a Ph.D. in the same subject four years later from the University of Minnesota. From 1935 until 1937 he carried out research at the University of Manchester, England, before being invited by physical chemist Gilbert Lewis (1875–1946) to become an instructor at the University of California at Berkeley. It was Lewis who introduced Calvin to the physicist Ernest Lawrence (1901–1958), winner of the 1939 Nobel Prize for Physics and director of the Radiation Laboratory at Berkeley.

Except for two years during World War II (1941–45) when he worked on the Manhattan Project at Los Alamos, New Mexico, Calvin remained at Berkeley for the rest of his career. His early research was on the study of organic molecules. A molecule consists of atoms linked by chemical bonds. "Organic" compounds are those that contain carbon; these form the basic material from which all living tissue is made.

### CARBON-14 ISOTOPES

In 1931 Lawrence had invented the cyclotron, a device that accelerates charged subatomic particles such as electrons, protons, and nuclei to high levels of energy. In 1940 physicists used the cyclotron to produce isotopes of radioactive carbon-14. Isotopes are atoms of an element that have the same number of positively charged protons in the nucleus but different numbers of neutrons, which carry no charge. Most elements are made up of a mixture of stable isotopes—they do not decompose readily. A few have naturally occurring radioactive isotopes. Carbon-14 (14C) is a radioactive carbon isotope produced by the impact of cosmic rays (charged

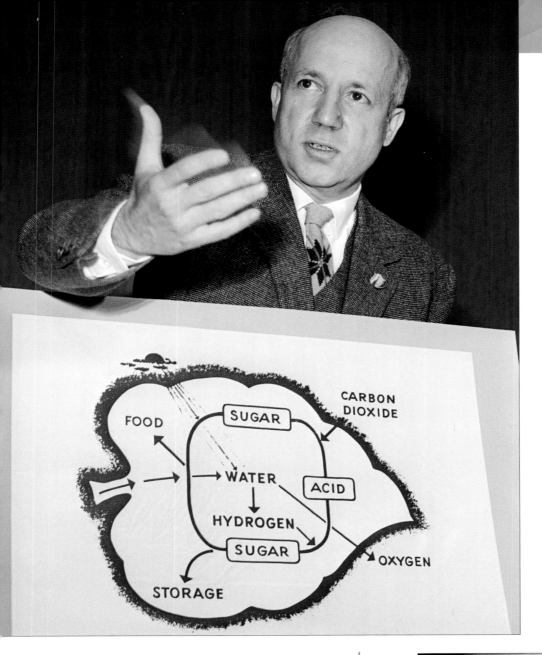

*Calvin (above) explains the process of photosynthesis with the aid of a diagram after winning the 1961 Nobel Prize for his work. Much of Calvin's career was spent working with the physicist Ernest Lawrence (right).*

particles) on nitrogen atoms in the atmosphere. The carbon-14 isotope can also be produced artificially by exposing stable carbon isotopes to radiation in an accelerator. Radioisotopes behave chemically and biologically in similar ways to stable isotopes. Their radiation can be easily monitored, so they can be used to "label" particular atoms or groups when studying

chemical reactions and biological processes. They have wide use in science, medicine, and industry.

## PHOTOSYNTHESIS REVEALED

In 1946 Lawrence suggested that Calvin work with carbon-14 isotopes, which were plentiful at the Radiation Laboratory. Calvin was made director of its

*A diagram (below) showing how photosynthesis works. Leaves and roots absorb the raw materials needed for the process, and energy from sunlight is also taken in by the plant. The plant gives off oxygen as a waste product. The equation (bottom) shows how carbon dioxide plus water is converted, using sunlight, into carbohydrates plus oxygen.*

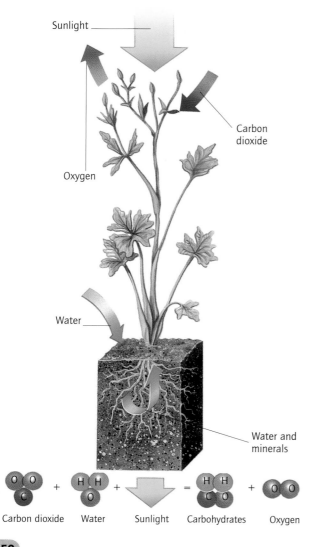

Sunlight

Carbon dioxide

Oxygen

Water

Water and minerals

Carbon dioxide    Water    Sunlight    Carbohydrates    Oxygen

Biological Division. In 1949 he began studying the chemical reactions that make up photosynthesis, the process by which green plants and some bacteria convert the energy of sunlight into chemical energy. Scientists already knew that photosynthesis occurs in two stages, then called the "light" and "dark" stages (now called "light-dependent" and "light-independent"). They knew that in the light stage a plant "captures" energy from sunlight, and that in the dark stage (which carries on in the absence of light) carbon dioxide combines with water to form organic compounds—sugars like glucose, for example—called carbohydrates. These are stored in roots and leaves and give the plant energy for growth and other living processes.

Calvin investigated the dark stage of photosynthesis by using carbon-14 to trace the movement of carbon through the reactions that convert carbon dioxide to sugars. By 1957 he was ready to describe the principal steps in what is now often referred to as "the Calvin cycle." Calvin also discovered that it is the action of sunlight on chlorophyll that drives photosynthesis. Chlorophyll is the green coloring matter in plants that absorbs light energy (see opposite).

## "LOLLIPOPS" PROVIDE THE ANSWER

Calvin identified the steps in the Calvin cycle using an apparatus resembling a "lollipop," consisting of a spherical flask mounted above a smaller flask. The complete apparatus was a series of such "lollipops."

The large flask contained a mixture (called a "suspension") of water, plant nutrient, and *Chlorella* (an algae). Algae are plants that have chlorophyll and other pigments but do not have proper stems, roots, or leaves. The group includes seaweeds. The suspension was poured in through the tube at the top, and air entered through another tube on the side. The carbon dioxide in the air was traced using carbon-14. The flask was exposed to bright light. The smaller flask contained methanol (methyl alcohol) and beneath it there was a source of heat. This kept the methanol gently boiling.

Supplied with light, water, and carbon dioxide, the algae carried out photosynthesis. At intervals varying from a few seconds to several minutes, a valve at the bottom of the flask was opened, allowing a small

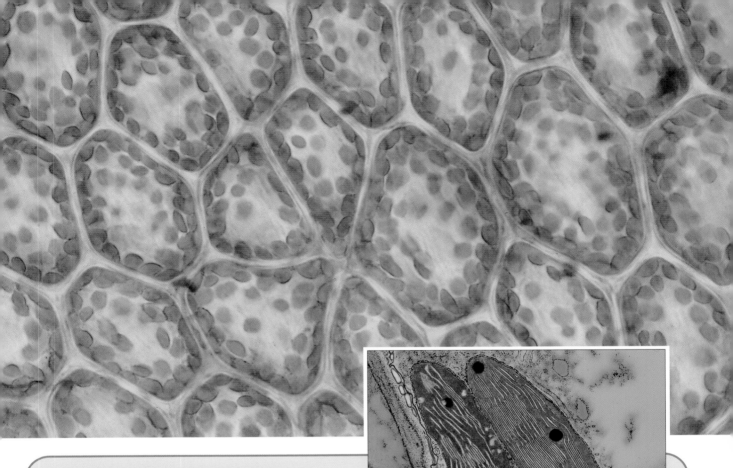

## CHLOROPLASTS AND CHLOROPHYLL

*M*ost living creatures, including humans, ultimately obtain the energy for their living processes from plant photosynthesis (exceptions are some bacteria that convert energy from hydrothermal vents, "black smokers," on the deep ocean bed, and the specialized creatures that feed off them). Plants use light energy and photosynthesis to make the sugars from which all other foods are made. Animals obtain energy by eating plants directly (herbivores) or by eating other animals that feed on plants (carnivores).

Plants can convert sunlight to food because their leaf cells contain structures called chloroplasts. Each chloroplast is a small bag that contains many other tiny, flattened membranes called thylakoids. The surfaces of the thylakoids are covered with chlorophyll, the green pigment that absorbs light energy in plants. A pigment has a special structure that lets it absorb light of a

*A close-up photograph shows a section through a leaf (main picture). The round structures in the cells are chloroplasts. The detail (above) shows two chloroplasts in the leaf of a pea plant (Pisum sativum). The flattened membranes, called thylakoids, contain the chlorophyll.*

particular color. The color of light is determined by its wavelength; chlorophyll absorbs light of red and blue-violet, so these wavelengths are most helpful for photosynthesis. The remainder of the light, mainly green, is reflected back by the chlorophyll, and that is why chlorophyll looks green. Chlorophyll absorbs light and releases electrons when it does so. It is these electrons that drive the chemical reactions of photosynthesis.

amount of the suspension to enter the tube. The boiling methanol and the heat quickly stopped the photosynthetic reactions of the algae. By tapping first one "lollipop" and then another it was possible to stop photosynthesis at different stages for study.

Compounds that had formed could be isolated because the carbon they contained had been traced using carbon-14. The compounds were then analyzed using paper chromatography (see below). This allowed Calvin to follow each of the steps by which glucose is produced during the light-independent stage of photosynthesis. Calvin began his experiments in 1949. He published his results in a book entitled *The Path of Carbon in Photosynthesis* in 1957.

## HONORED FOR HIS ACHIEVEMENTS

For his work on photosynthesis, Calvin received many awards and honors, including the Nobel Prize for chemistry in 1961 and the U.S. National Medal of Science in 1989. Later Calvin turned his attention to the possibility of using photosynthesis in oil-producing plants to produce fuel substitutes. He was also interested in the chemical evolution of life, especially the part played by photosynthesis in this process.

## PAPER CHROMATOGRAPHY

Melvin Calvin used paper chromatography as a method of identifying the products produced during the various stages of photosynthesis. Paper chromatography was a technique that had been developed by British biochemists Archer Martin (1910–2002) and Richard Synge (1914–1994), who were awarded the 1952 Nobel Prize for chemistry for their achievement.

Paper chromatography makes use of absorbent paper, such as filter paper or blotting paper. A spot of the liquid mixture to be analyzed is placed near one edge of a sheet of the paper and allowed to dry. The paper is then held upright with its bottom edge dipping into a trough containing a solvent—a substance that can dissolve another, such as an alcohol. The solvent creeps slowly up the paper. As it passes the spot of mixture, the component parts of the mixture dissolve in the solvent and also pass up the paper. But the components move at different rates, depending on how soluble they are. The most soluble components travel farthest.

The paper is then dried, and the different components form a row of spots along the paper. By measuring the distance each component has moved in a certain time, analysts can identify each substance. This is made possible by comparing the results against previous separations carried out with known substances. Using microanalysis, it is also possible to find out how much of a component there is in a particular spot.

*Paper chromatography was developed in 1941. Today it is still a vital tool in biochemical and molecular research.*

# MELVIN CALVIN

## SCIENTIFIC BACKGROUND

**Before 1940**

Scientists establish that photosynthesis (the process by which plants convert light energy into chemical energy) occurs in two stages, the "light" (now known as "light-dependent") and "dark"

In Berkeley, California, Ernest Lawrence (1901–1958) develops a device that accelerates particles to create radioactive isotopes, including carbon-14

**1941** British biochemists Archer Martin (1910–2002) and Richard Synge (1914–1994) develop paper chromatography

**1946** Lawrence suggests that Calvin should begin working with carbon-14

**1949** Calvin begins to investigate the chemical steps involved in photosynthesis

**1952** Martin and Synge win the Nobel Prize for chemistry for their development of the technique of paper chromatography

**1957** Calvin publishes his findings, describing the main steps in what is now known as the "Calvin cycle"

**1961** Calvin is awarded the Nobel Prize for chemistry for his work on photosynthesis

**1969** Calvin publishes his book, *Chemical Evolution*, exploring conditions for the origin of life

**1971** Calvin becomes professor of chemistry at the University of California, Berkeley

**After 1980**

**1982** Calvin proposes oil-producing plants as a source of renewable energy

**1988** German biochemists Johann Deisenhofer (1943– ), Robert Huber (1937– ), and Hartmut Michel (1948– ) win the Nobel Prize for chemistry for their work on the structure of certain proteins that are essential for photosynthesis

---

**1940**  **1950**  **1960**  **1970**

---

## POLITICAL AND CULTURAL BACKGROUND

**1941** World War II (1939–45) becomes a genuinely global conflict as Germany invades the Soviet Union and Japan attacks the U.S. Navy's Pacific fleet at Pearl Harbor, Hawaii

**1946** At an address in Fulton, Missouri, former British prime minister Winston Churchill (1874–1965) coins the term "Iron Curtain" for the boundary between Communist Eastern Europe and capitalist Western Europe

**1952** In Argentina millions mourn the death of first lady Eva Perón from cancer at the age of 33

**1956** The first United Nations peacekeeping force occupies the Suez Canal Zone. Egypt's nationalization of the canal has prompted military intervention by Britain, France, and Israel to protect the shipping route

**1959** The revolutionary Marxist government of Fidel Castro (1926– ) takes power in Cuba

**1963** On August 28 nearly 250,000 black Americans join the "March on Washington" to demand civil rights

**1965** In an attempt to prevent Communist North Vietnam winning power in South Vietnam, by August the United States have an army of 125,000 men on active service in Vietnam; within the next year the figure will rise to nearly 400,000

**1970** Four students die at Kent State University in Ohio when National Guardsmen fire on anti-Vietnam War protesters

**1972** In a relaxation of Cold War tensions, President Richard M. Nixon (1913–1994) visits Beijing to open diplomatic relations with Communist China

**1977** Star Wars, an American science-fiction film that stars Harrison Ford (1942– ) and Mark Hamill (1951– ), and is directed by George Lucas (1944– ), proves a huge and enduring hit around the world

# FRANCIS CRICK, ROSALIND FRANKLIN, AND JAMES WATSON

1916–2004, 1920–1958, 1928–

*" Wilkins and Franklin gave Crick and Watson their data. Nobody else in the world had that data... The Crick-Watson discovery of the double helix...was the result of having a good tool with which to analyze the DNA molecule."*

Freeman Dyson (1923– )
*English born American physicist*

THE WORK OF ENGLISH X-RAY CRYSTALLOGRAPHER ROSALIND FRANKLIN, ENGLISH MOLECULAR BIOLOGIST FRANCIS CRICK, AND AMERICAN BIOLOGIST JAMES D. WATSON LED TO THE DISCOVERY OF DEOXYRIBONUCLEIC ACID (DNA), THE SUBSTANCE THAT MAKES UP OUR GENES. THEIR WORK ALSO MADE POSSIBLE AN UNDERSTANDING OF DNA'S STRUCTURE AND HOW IT COPIES ITSELF. SCIENTISTS HAVE NOW LISTED NEARLY ALL THE GENES IN THE HUMAN BODY, WHICH SHOULD LEAD TO BETTER PREVENTION AND TREATMENT OF DISEASES.

Rosalind Franklin was born in London on July 25, 1920. She graduated in chemistry and physics in 1941, and in 1942 she joined the British Coal Utilization Research Association to do war work. In 1945 Cambridge University awarded her a Ph.D. in physical chemistry. In 1947 Franklin moved to Paris to work at the Central Government Laboratory for Chemistry, where she learned X-ray diffraction (also known as X-ray crystallography) techniques. These would prove vital in the search for the structure of the DNA molecule. Molecules are far too small to examine under a microscope. Chemists can work out from the rules of chemistry how each atom is attached to its neighbors. What they cannot work out is the final shape of a molecule, which can contain hundreds of atoms.

## CRYSTAL STRUCTURE

X-ray crystallography can reveal a molecule's shape. A crystal is an arrangement of regularly spaced atoms. If X-rays pass through a crystal, each of the atoms in the crystal bends the X-ray beam in a characteristic way caused by the density of electrons in each atom. Electrons are particles with negative charge that surround each atom's nucleus.

X-rays expose photographic film, so if a piece of film is placed behind the crystal, the deflected X-rays form a pattern of spots that appear when the film is developed. The pattern reveals the density of the electrons in each part of the picture. Knowing the electron density allows scientists to calculate the position of each atom in the crystal. This can be plotted as a computer graphic or used to build a model.

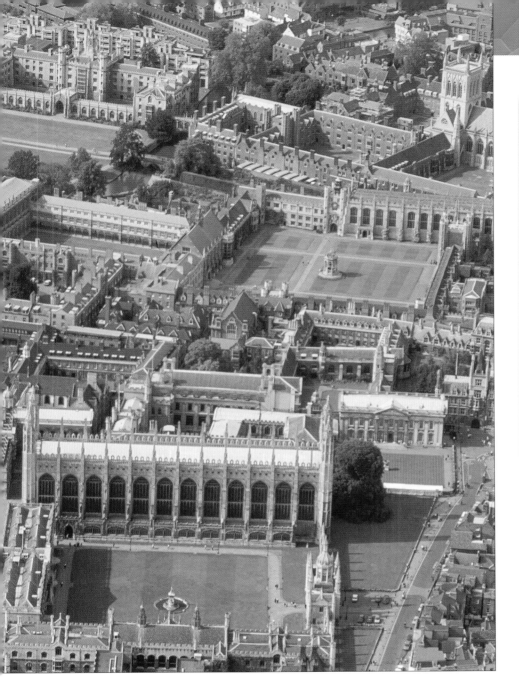

## KEY DATES

**1949** Crick joins the Medical Research Council unit at the Cavendish Laboratory, Cambridge

**1951** Watson goes to work at the Cavendish Laboratory and meets Crick; Watson learns X-ray diffraction techniques and works with Crick on the problem of DNA structure

**1951–53** Franklin joins a research group at King's College, London, under Maurice Wilkins, working on X-ray diffraction of DNA

**1953** Wilkins shows Franklin's DNA photographs to Crick and Watson, who publish their discovery of the structure of DNA on April 25

**1962** Crick, Watson, and Wilkins receive the Nobel Prize for physiology or medicine

**1977** Crick is Kieckhofer Professor at the Salk Institute for Biological Studies in San Diego, California

**1989** Watson is made director of the National Center for Human Genome Research and launches the Human Genome Project

*Part of Cambridge University, England. Franklin graduated from Cambridge, Crick was a research student there, and Crick and Watson carried out their work on the structure of DNA at the university's Cavendish Laboratories.*

In 1951 Franklin became a research associate in the biophysics research laboratory at King's College, London. There she met Maurice Wilkins (1916–2004), assistant director of the laboratory. Franklin and Wilkins worked on examining the DNA molecule.

## THE NATURE OF DNA

New individuals resemble their parents. If you plant an acorn it will grow into an oak tree and never an elm tree. Cats give birth to kittens and never to puppies. In 1865 biologist Gregor Mendel (1822–1884) presented a paper in which he described experiments he had conducted with pea plants. Mendel had discovered the way particular characteristics are transmitted from parents to their offspring by means of what he called "heritable factors."

*James Watson (right) and Francis Crick (far right), in 1953. Behind them are the "ball-and-spoke" models that they used to determine molecular structure, and in particular the shape of the DNA molecule.*

In 1882 the German biologist Walther Flemming (1843–1905) described seeing these "heritable factors" as short, threadlike objects that he called "chromosomes." Ten years later the German zoologist August Friedrich Leopold Weismann (1834–1914) proposed that every living organism contains "germ plasm," a substance that controls the development of every part of the body and is passed from parents to offspring. Weismann also realized that if germ plasm from both parents is mixed at fertilization, the amount of it must increase from one generation to the next. Since this does not happen, there must be cell division in which the resulting cells receive only half the full amount of germ plasm.

This was confirmed by another German biologist, Wilhelm August Oskar Hertwig (1849–1922). In 1875 Hertwig had described the fertilization of a sea urchin egg and also the type of cell division proposed by Weismann in which the amount of germ plasm is halved. This reduction-division process is called meiosis. In 1946 it was found that "germ plasm" is made from a nucleic acid called deoxyribonucleic acid, or DNA. We now know that genes (DNA) direct the cell to assemble proteins. These proteins give us our individual features.

Franklin designed a camera that provided images of DNA that had been stretched into a thin fiber. She was the first to report that the sugar-phosphate backbone of DNA lies on the outside of the DNA molecule. Her photographs showed that DNA might be arranged as a helix—a spiral shape, like a screw thread.

### CRICK AND WATSON MAKE THE DOUBLE HELIX

Franklin was close to discovering the structure of DNA, but two other people would prove vital to the outcome.

Francis Harry Crick was born on June 8, 1916, in England. In 1937 he graduated with a degree in physics from University College, London. He then went to work for the British Admiralty. In 1949 he joined the Medical Research Council unit at the Cavendish Laboratory, Cambridge, where he worked on X-ray diffraction of proteins. He was awarded his Ph.D. in 1953.

James Dewey Watson was born on April 6, 1928, in Chicago, Illinois. He graduated in zoology at Chicago University in 1947, and in 1950 he was awarded his Ph.D. in zoology at Indiana University. His interest in the huge diversity of birds led him to study genetics. Eminent geneticists in the bacteriology department at Indiana University guided him in his doctoral research into the effect of X-rays on the multiplication of bacteriophages (viruses that attack bacteria). Watson became convinced that the chemical structure of genes was of fundamental biological importance.

Watson began investigating the structural chemistry of nucleic acids and proteins, and learned that scientists were using photographs of X-ray diffraction patterns of protein crystals to study protein molecule structure. In 1951 he moved to the Cavendish Laboratory, Cambridge, where he began working with Francis Crick on the problem of the structure of DNA. Crick had experience with X-ray diffraction, and Watson understood genetics and biochemistry. It was at this time that Maurice Wilkins showed Crick and Watson the photographs of the X-ray diffraction patterns made by DNA crystals that Franklin had taken.

Crick and Watson were convinced that if the structure of DNA were known, then its role in heredity would become clear. Helped by the X-ray diffraction studies passed to them by Wilkins, they made a model of DNA based on its known properties. They realized that the DNA molecule must be arranged in a double spiral, like two long twisting ladders wound around each other—a "double helix" construction. Eventually Crick and Watson were able to show how a molecule consisting of two helixes running in opposite directions could separate into single strands and how each strand could then assemble a complementary strand. They described their findings in two papers published in the British scientific journal *Nature* in April and May, 1953.

## FURTHER WORK

Rosalind Franklin later studied viruses. Tragically, she died of cancer in 1958. Nobel Prizes are not awarded after death, so she did not share in the Nobel Prize for physiology or medicine that Crick, Watson, and Wilkins received in 1962 for their work on DNA.

Crick did further important work on the "genetic code," the sequence of bases in DNA that provide the instructions for the production of proteins, and helped identify the groups of three bases (codons) that form the approximately 20 amino acids that make up proteins. In 1977 he became professor at the Salk Institute for Biological Studies in San Diego, California.

Watson returned to the United States in 1953 to research into ribonucleic acid (RNA) at the California Institute of Technology. In 1955 he returned to the Cavendish Laboratory and worked with Crick on the

## GENETIC FINGERPRINTING

Identifying criminals is one task that has been made dramatically easier by genetic finger-printing. The technique is based on the fact that each human—with the exception of identical twins—has a unique genetic makeup.

In order to identify a "fingerprint," a DNA sample is taken from the scene of the crime: hair, blood, and saliva are suitable sources. The samples are place on a paper soaked in a solution that will conduct electricity but not alter the sample. An electric current is passed through the solution and the DNA moves through it. This is known as "electrophoresis." If samples that are placed side by side travel the same distance, they are identical and from the same person. If they travel different distances, they are from different people.

The first criminal conviction based on DNA testing was in the United States in 1988. The use of genetic fingerprinting in criminal cases is now widespread. By 2007 the Federal Bureau of Investigation had a national database of more than 5 million DNA profiles. While supporters of the technique argue that it protects the innocent, others are uneasy about its use. There are concerns about how controlled and accurate testing methods are, as well as ethical concerns about whether people should have to produce samples of DNA when they are only suspected of a crime.

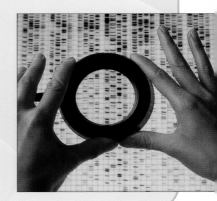

*After electrophoresis, radioactive markers are used to bind with the DNA. The DNA bands react with X-ray film. Here an operative is holding a computer scanner to read and compare samples.*

structure of viruses. In 1961 he became professor of the Biology Department at Harvard, and in 1968, director of the Cold Spring Harbor Laboratory on Long Island, New York. In 1989 he was appointed director of the National Center for Human Genome Research. In 1994 he became president of Cold Spring Harbor Laboratory, guiding research into the molecular basis of cancer.

## DNA STRUCTURE

Discovering DNA's structure has been described as the key to understanding the chemistry of reproduction— the characteristic that most readily distinguishes the living from the nonliving world. DNA had been isolated in the 19th century, but it was another 60 years before evidence emerged that it was the molecule of inheritance. Proof came in 1944 when American bacteriologist Oswald Avery (1877–1955) showed that the DNA isolated from one strain of bacterium could alter the appearance of a second strain by mixing the DNA of the first with the cells of the second.

Chemical analysis had already shown that DNA is a polymer (long repeating chain) made up of a backbone of sugar and phosphate atoms. Four nitrogenous (nitrogen-containing) "bases" are attached to the sugar. These are chemical units called cytosine (C), thymine (T), adenine (A), and guanine (G). Cytosine and thymine differ in their molecular structure from adenine and guanine, so the bases form two groups. Cytosine and thymine are pyrimidines. Adenine and guanine are purines. Watson and Crick discovered that the bases link to each other, but only in a particular way: a pyrimidine will link only with a purine, so cytosine and guanine will link together and thymine and adenine will link together.

## HOW DNA REPLICATES ITSELF

The specific pairing suggested how the molecule could replicate (copy itself). How it does this is the key to its role as the molecule of inheritance. DNA forms a double helix, meaning there are two long molecules twisted around one another. The sugar-phosphate backbone is on the outside of the helix and the bases are on the inside. DNA is contained in chromosomes in the nucleus of every cell. When a cell divides into two,

its DNA, is copied, so each of the new cells has its own DNA, and the DNA is identical in both cells.

First, the double helix straightens out (see diagram opposite). Untwisted, the DNA is shaped like a ladder, with the two sugar-phosphate backbones forming the sides of the ladder and the bases forming the rungs. The DNA molecule gradually splits in two; the pairs of bases separate and the two strands part. Each strand has a row of the four different types of single bases joined to it (shown opposite as green, red, blue, and yellow), which will only bond with their appropriate opposite numbers. The bases bond with bases of free nucleotide units to form a pair of identical DNA molecules. The process is controlled by enzymes. More sugar and phosphate groups join the bases to make a new backbone. Each single strand has assembled its own partner, making the two double strands identical.

The nitrogenous bases of DNA instruct the cell to make protein molecules. Some of these are used to build or repair the cell, some help with the chemical reactions that keep the cell working, and some turn genes on or off (for example, activating genes governing sexual maturity when humans reach puberty).

## GENETIC ENGINEERING

When bacteria defend themselves against attack by bacteriophages (viruses that attack bacteria), they use enzymes to cut the bacteriophage DNA at specific points in its chain. These "restriction enzymes," gave scientists a way to retrieve sections of DNA, which could be stored, transferred, or rearranged between organisms. This is called genetic engineering.

Genetic engineering opened the way to many developments. Biochemists can now produce genetically modified (G.M.) crops, for example, in which the gene that makes one species resistant to a particular pest or disease can be transferred to another species. In medicine, genetic engineering may come to be used to combat a number of genetically acquired diseases by altering the genes responsible. However, there are serious concerns about not just the medical but also the ethical risks of the technique: many people are fearful of how far scientists should be permitted to go in interfering with the blueprint of life.

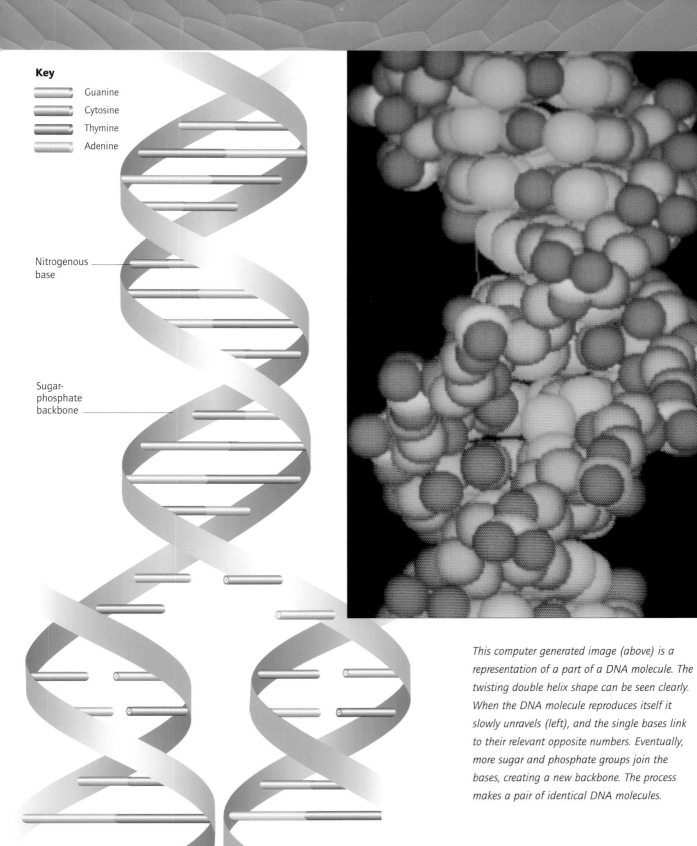

**Key**

Guanine
Cytosine
Thymine
Adenine

Nitrogenous
base

Sugar-
phosphate
backbone

This computer generated image (above) is a representation of a part of a DNA molecule. The twisting double helix shape can be seen clearly. When the DNA molecule reproduces itself it slowly unravels (left), and the single bases link to their relevant opposite numbers. Eventually, more sugar and phosphate groups join the bases, creating a new backbone. The process makes a pair of identical DNA molecules.

# FRANCIS CRICK, ROSALIND FRANKLIN, AND JAMES WATSON

## SCIENTIFIC BACKGROUND

**Before 1940**

Austrian biologist Gregor Mendel (1822–1884) presents a paper describing "heritable factors"

German biologist Walther Flemming (1843–1905) reveals chromosomes

German zoologist August Weismann (1834–1914) reports germ plasm

Wilhelm Hertwig (1849–1922), a German biologist, first describes reduction cell division (meiosis)

X-ray crystallography is developed by father and son British physicists W. H. Bragg (1862–1942) and W. L. Bragg (1890–1971)

**1944** American bacteriologist Oswald Avery (1877–1955) shows that DNA isolated from one bacterium can alter the appearance of a second strain

**1946** New Zealander Maurice Wilkins (1916–2004) works on the structure of DNA at King's College, London

**1946** British chemist Dorothy Hodgkin (1910–1994) unravels the complex structure of the antibiotic drug penicillin using X-ray crystallography

**1947** Franklin works at the Central Government Laboratory for Chemistry in Paris, France, on X-ray diffraction techniques

**1949** Crick joins the Medical Research Council at the Cavendish Laboratory, Cambridge, to work on X-ray diffraction

**1951** Watson begins to investigate the structural chemistry of nucleic acids and proteins and teams up with Crick

**1953** Wilkins shows Franklin's DNA photographs to Watson and Crick, who publish their discovery of the structure of DNA on April 25

## 1940 · 1945 · 1950

## POLITICAL AND CULTURAL BACKGROUND

**1940** Tenzin Gyatso (1935– ) is enthroned as the 14th Dalai Lama, the spiritual leader of Tibet

**1943** As World War II (1939–45) continues, in the Pacific the U.S. navy begins a campaign of "island-hopping" toward Japan—using one island after another as a base for capturing the next

**1945** In Italy, fascist leader Benito Mussolini (1883–1945) is captured, tried, and executed by partisans while trying to escape to Switzerland

**1947** The U.S. State Department begins the Voice of America radio station, broadcasting to the Soviet Union in Russian

**1950** On July 25 troops from North Korea suddenly invade South Korea, starting a war that will involve troops from 15 United Nations (U.N.) member countries; an armistice is declared on July 27, 1953 but no formal peace treaty is ever signed

**1950** The musical *Guys and Dolls* opens in New York. With songs by Frank Loesser (1910–1969), it will become one of Broadway's best-loved shows

**1955** Watson becomes assistant professor at Harvard University

**1958** Franklin dies of cancer

**1959** British virologist Hugh Cairns (1922– ) succeeds in carrying out the genetic mapping of an animal virus for the first time

**1959** Crick is a visiting professor at Harvard University

**1962** Crick, Watson, and Wilkins receive the Nobel Prize for physiology or medicine

**1968** Watson publishes his account of the discovery of the structure of DNA, *The Double Helix*

**1968** Watson becomes director of Cold Spring Harbor laboratory, Long Island, N.Y.

**1969** Researchers identify the beginning of a single gene in strands of DNA

**1973** As a result of work done by American biologists Daniel Nathans (1928–1999) and Hamilton Smith (1931– ) on restriction enzymes, scientists succeed in implanting a gene into a bacterium

**After 1975**

**1980** American molecular biologists Paul Berg (1926– ), Walter Gilbert (1932– ), and British biochemist Frederick Sanger (1918– ) share the Nobel Prize for chemistry for their work on nucleic acids

**1990** The Human Genome Project is set up to construct a map of human genetic composition

**1990** Gene therapy on a human being is carried out for the first time

**2001** A working draft of the human genome is published

---

**1955** | **1960** | **1965** | **1970** | **1975**

---

**1958** In France the proposals by General Charles de Gaulle (1890–1970) that the president should have wider powers are approved by referendum; de Gaulle becomes the first president of the Fifth Republic

**1960** Democratic senator John F. Kennedy (1917–1963) defeats Republican Richard Nixon (1913–1994) to become the youngest person to be elected U.S. president

**1963** Tamla Motown releases the first album by blind singer Steveland Judkins (1950– ) under his stage name; it is called *Little Stevie Wonder: the 12-year-old Genius*

**1964** American boxer Cassius Clay (1942– ) wins the world heavyweight boxing championship; he announces his conversion to Islam and adopts the name Muhammad Ali

**1967** In China the People's Liberation Army moves to restore order and the authority of the Communist Party as Red Guards rampage through the country

**1967** South African surgeon Christiaan Barnard (1922–2001) performs the first human heart transplant

**1971** The 26th Amendment to the U.S. Constitution gives 18-year-olds the right to vote

**1972** Soviet gymnast Olga Korbut (1955– ) wins three gold medals and one silver and becomes the darling of the Olympic Games held in Munich, Germany

# GLOSSARY

**Amino acids** An important class of organic (carbon-containing) compounds.

**Anatomy** The structure and form of biological organisms.

**Anthropology** The study of humans from biological, cultural, and social viewpoints.

**Antibiotic** A substance that kills or prevents the growth of other microorganisms. They include penicillins; they are used in the treatment of infection by bacteria or fungi.

**Antibodies and antigens** Antibodies are defense proteins made by some white cells in the body to counter invading proteins known as antigens. Antibodies bind to antigens, tagging them for destruction by phagocytes (white blood cells that destroy invading bodies), or by activating a chemical system that makes the antigen harmless.

**Antiseptic** A substance that prevents the growth or spread of microorganisms.

**Archeology** The study of the past through identification and interpretation of the material remains of human cultures.

**Bacteria** Single-celled microorganisms. Some exist harmlessly alongside host cells; others live in cells or body cavities and produce toxins that damage the host.

**Bacteriology** The science that deals with bacteria, their characteristics, and activities.

**Bacteriophage** A virus that attacks bacteria.

**Base pairing** The process that holds together the strands of double-stranded DNA and, in the case of some viruses, double-stranded RNA. Base pairs always contain one pyrimidine and one purine.

**Biochemistry** The study of substances in living organisms and the chemical reactions in which they are involved.

**Biology** The study of living things. There are many branches of biology, such as botany, ecology, genetics, microbiology, and zoology.

**Botany** The scientific study of plant life.

**Cell** In biology, the unit of living matter from which almost all organisms are built.

**Cell nucleus** The central compartment of a cell that contains the chromosomes and associated molecules that control the characteristics and growth of the cell.

**Chromosome** Threadlike structures that carry the genetic information in the form of DNA, and contain various proteins.

**Deoxyribonucleic acid (DNA)** A large complex molecule—a double-stranded nucleic acid—that forms the basis of genetic inheritance in almost all living organisms.

**Enzyme** A protein that acts as a catalyst to speed up chemical reactions in converting one molecule into another.

**Evolution** The process by which organisms have changed since the origin of life.

**Fermentation** The breakdown of glucose and other sugars by bacteria or yeasts in the absence of oxygen.

**Fossil** The remains of an animal, plant, or other organism preserved in rocks.

**Gene** The basic unit of inheritance that controls a characteristic of an organism.

**Genetic code** The means by which genetic information is translated into the molecules that make up living organisms.

**Genetic engineering** The manipulation of genetic material. The purpose can be research into cell function and reproduction, or to breed organisms. Genetic engineering has been used, for example, to produce crops that are resistant to disease.

**Genetics** The study of inheritance and its units (genes).

**Germ** A common term for a microorganism capable of causing disease.

**Immunity** The ability to resist infection by viruses, bacteria, and other disease-causing microorganisms.

**Immunization** The process of conferring immunity, particularly by inoculation.

**Inoculation** The injection or introduction of microorganisms or their products into living tissues in order to produce immunity.

**Microorganism** Any single-celled organism that can only be seen with a microscope.

**Organic chemistry** The branch of chemistry that deals with carbon compounds. Organic compounds form the basic stuff of living tissue.

**Organism** Any living animal or plant, including any bacterium or virus.

**Paleontology** The study of ancient life, including the structure of organisms, their environment and evolution, as shown by fossils.

**Parasite** An organism that is for some part of its life history dependent on another, the "host," from which it obtains nutrition.

**Pasteurization** A process involving the controlled heating of beverages or foods in order to destroy harmful microorganisms or to limit the rate at which the product ferments. It is used in the food industry: milk is usually pasteurized, for example.

**Photosynthesis** The process by which green plants use light energy to produce sugar (a compound of carbon and hydrogen) from carbon dioxide and water.

**Physiology** The study of function in living organisms.

**Replication** The production of exact copies of complex molecules, such as DNA.

**Reproduction** The process by which an organism produces its offspring.

**Respiration** Sometimes used to mean breathing, respiration is actually the sequence of reactions in living cells that break down foods to yield energy.

**Ribonucleic acid (RNA)** A nucleic acid that is concerned with protein synthesis. In some viruses RNA is the hereditary material. RNA carries information from DNA to the site where amino acids are assembled into proteins.

**Species** A group of living organisms that can interbreed to produce fertile offspring.

**Taxonomy** The branch of biology concerned with classification of living organisms into groups.

**Toxin** A poisonous substance produced by a living organism. Toxins play an important part in defense and the killing of prey.

**Vaccination** Method of giving immunity against infectious disease caused by bacteria or viruses.

**Viruses** Tiny parasitic organisms that can reproduce only inside the cell of their host. Viruses replicate by invading host cells and taking over the cell's machinery for DNA replication and protein synthesis.

**Zoology** The scientific study of animal life.

# FURTHER RESOURCES

## PUBLICATIONS

### ANTHROPOLOGY, EVOLUTION, AND GENETICS

Beatty, Richard. *Genetics.* Austin, Texas: Raintree Steck-Vaughn, 2001.

Crapo, Richley H. *Cultural Anthropology: Understanding Ourselves and Others.* Boston: McGraw-Hill, 2002.

Edelson, Edward. *Francis Crick and James Watson and the Building Blocks of Life.* New York: Oxford University Press, 1998.

Eriksen, Thomas Hylland, and Finn Sivert Nielsen. *A History of Anthropology.* Sterling, Va.: Pluto Press, 2001.

Gardner, Robert. *Human Evolution.* New York: Franklin Watts, 1999.

Klare, Roger. *Gregor Mendel: Father of Genetics.* Springfield, NJ: Enslow, 1997.

Nardo, Don. *Origin of Species: Darwin's Theory of Evolution.* San Diego, CA: Lucent, 2001.

Podolefsky, Aaron, and Peter J. Brown, eds. *Applying Anthropology: An Introductory Reader.* Columbus, OH: McGraw-Hill, 2008.

Strathern, Paul. *Crick, Watson, and DNA.* New York: Anchor Books, 1999.

Watson, James D. *The Double Helix: A Personal Account of the Discovery of the Structure of DNA.* New York: Scribner, 1998.

### BIOCHEMISTRY, BIOLOGY, AND ENVIRONMENTAL SCIENCE

Anderson, Margaret J. *Charles Darwin, Naturalist.* Hillside, NJ: Enslow, 2001.

Calvin, Melvin. *Following the Trail of Light: A Scientific Odyssey.* Washington, D.C.: American Chemical Society, 1992.

Magner, Lois N. *A History of the Life Sciences.* 2nd ed. New York: M. Dekker, 1994.

Milner, Richard. *Charles Darwin: Evolution of a Naturalist.* New York: Facts on File, 1994.

Raven, P.H., L.R. Berg, and D.M. Hassenzahl. *Environment.* Hoboken,NJ: John Wiley & Sons, 2008.

### MEDICINE

Friedman, Meyer, and Gerald W. Friedland. *Medicine's 10 Greatest Discoveries.* New Haven, CT: Yale University Press, 2000.

Gottfried, Ted. *Alexander Fleming: Discoverer of Penicillin.* New York: Franklin Watts, 1997.

Harding, Anne S. *Milestones in Health and Medicine.* Phoenix: Oryx, 2000.

Robbins, Louise. *Louis Pasteur and the Hidden World of Microbes.* New York: Oxford University Press, 2001.

Royston, Angela. *100 Greatest Medical Discoveries.* Danbury, CT: Grolier Educational, 1997.

Smith, Linda Wasmer. *Louis Pasteur: Disease Fighter.* Springfield, NJ: Enslow, 2001.

Yount, Lisa. *History of Medicine.* San Diego, CA.: Lucent Books, 2001.

### PALEONTOLOGY

Cowen, Richard. *History of Life.* Malden, MA.: Blackwell Science, 2000.

Erickson, Jon. *Lost Creatures of the Earth: Mass Extinction in the History of Life.* New York: Facts on File, 2001.

Fairbridge, Rhodes W., and David Jablonski, eds. *The Encyclopedia of Paleontology.* Stroudsburg, PA.: Dowden, Hutchinson & Ross, 1979.

Knight, Charles R. *Life Through the Ages.* Bloomington, IN: Indiana University Press, 2001.

Lambert, David. *Encyclopedia of Prehistory.* New York: Facts on File, 2002.

Lambert, Lisa A. *The Leakeys.* Vero Beach, FL: Rourke, 1993.

Lasky, Kathryn. *Traces of Life: The Origins of Humankind.* New York: Morrow Junior, 1989.

Leakey, R. E. *The Origin of Humankind.* New York: Basic Books,1996.

Pickford, Martin. *Louis S. B. Leakey: Beyond the Evidence.* London: Janus, 1997.

Poynter, Margaret. *The Leakeys: Uncovering the Origins of Humankind.* Springfield, NJ: Enslow, 1997.

Reader's Digest Association. *Life Before Man.* New York: Reader's Digest Association, 1997.

Taquet, Philippe. *Dinosaur Impressions: Postcards from a Paleontologist.* Trans. Kevin Padian. New York: Cambridge University Press, 1999.

Willis, Delta. *The Leakey Family: Leaders in the Search for Human Origins.* New York: Facts on File, 1992.

## WEBSITES

### ANTHROPOLOGY, EVOLUTION, AND GENETICS

*The Field Museum*
www.fmnh.org
Includes online exhibits on topics ranging from best-preserved fossil of Tyrannosaurus found, to ancient musical instruments and underground exploration.

*Minnesota State University E-Museum*
http://www.mnsu.edu/emuseum/index.shtml
Virtual anthropology and archaeology museum, covering cultural anthropology, evolution, human cultures, paleontology, and more.

*The Talk.Origins Archive*
www.talkorigins.org
Articles discussing aspects of the evolution/creationism debate.

*University of California Museum of Paleontology Evolution Wing*
www.ucmp.berkeley.edu/history/evolution.html
Exploration of evolutionary theory. Includes a timeline of evolutionary thought and biographies of researchers in the natural sciences, explanation of phylogeny, and sections about dinosaurs.

*Primer on Molecular Genetics*
http://www.ornl.gov/sci/techresources/Human_Genome/public at/primer/toc.html
Offers a comprehensive review of the basic concepts of genetics and fairly detailed information about the human genome project.

### BIOLOGY

*The Biology Project*
www.biology.arizona.edu
Interactive online resource for learning biology developed at the University of Arizona.

### MEDICINE

*Medicine Through Time*
http://www.bbc.co.uk/schools/gcsebitesize/history/shp/
Descriptions of medical technology through the ages, including topics in disease treatment, surgery, hospitals, and public health.

*From Quackery to Bacteriology: The Emergence of Modern Medicine in 19th Century America*
http://www.utoledo.edu/library/canaday/exhibits/quackery/quack1.html
Development of medicine in the United States from heroic medicine and quackery to germ theory at the turn of the twentieth century.

### PALEONTOLOGY

*Becoming Human*
www.becominghuman.org
Interactive online film documentary about the story of human evolution.

*Strange Science: The Rocky Road to Modern Paleontology and Biology*
http://www.strangescience.net/
A timeline of the history of paleontology, biographies of notable paleontologists, stories of notable mistakes, and absurd theories.

# INDEX

Bold page numbers
indicate a major article
about the subject.